# The Inner Warrior

# THE INNER
# WARRIOR

## Developing Courage for Personal and Organizational Change

Beverley Stone

palgrave
macmillan

First published 2004 by
PALGRAVE MACMILLAN
Houndmills, Basingstoke, Hampshire RG21 6XS and
175 Fifth Avenue, New York, N.Y. 10010
Companies and representatives throughout the world

PALGRAVE MACMILLAN is the global academic imprint of the Palgrave Macmillan division of St. Martin's Press, LLC and of Palgrave Macmillan Ltd. Macmillan® is a registered trademark in the United States, United Kingdom and other countries. Palgrave is a registered trademark in the European Union and other countries.

ISBN 1–4039–3677–3

This book is printed on paper suitable for recycling and made from fully managed and sustained forest sources.

A catalogue record for this book is available from the British Library.

A catalog record for this book is available from the Library of Congress.

10  9  8  7  6  5  4  3  2  1
13 12 11 10 09 08 07 06 05 04

Printed and bound in China

*To my mother, Lulu Stone, and my daughters, Zelda and Becky*
*whose connection to their Inner Warrior makes them*
*masters of authenticity, compassion and courage.*

# CONTENTS

# Contents

# LIST OF FIGURES AND TABLES

## Figures

## Tables

# PREFACE

## THE PURPOSE OF THE BOOK AND HOW IT DIFFERS FROM OTHERS

This book is aimed at everyone who wants to make both themselves and their organization healthier: healthier in human terms, healthier in business terms.

In every organization there are hidden barriers to optimum performance. People are not contributing fully because they are unconsciously or consciously marginalized by others. These barriers are derived from the organization's culture, the team dynamics and personal and interpersonal experiences. This book will show you how to remove them.

Many current training and development methods aimed at removing barriers are failing. Even the ones that are theoretically sound are short lived in their effect.

The purpose of the book is to effect real change in people so that these personal, interpersonal and group barriers no longer exist and talented people can thrive.

It will clarify what goes wrong in the implementation of many management theories and change programmes. The book argues that *courage* is a necessary component of all change.

Organizations acknowledge that success can only be achieved when people learn to:

- express themselves
- challenge assumptions
- be innovative
- take risks and try out new ways of doing things
- confront vested interests
- win over the sceptics
- disagree openly and honestly
- manage their careers
- do what is right for the organization

Yet, all too often the development programmes that exist do not achieve these desired results.

The missing component is courage:

- the courage to be unafraid to express themselves
- the courage to challenge assumptions
- the courage to be innovative
- the courage to take risks and try out new ways of doing things
- the courage to confront vested interests
- the courage to win over the sceptics
- the courage to disagree openly and honestly
- the courage to manage their careers
- the courage to do what is right for the organization

The expectations of many programmes of change are that people will return with such courage. But most people do not.

## THE INNER WARRIOR AND ITS OUTER COUNTERPART

Developing that courage is no easy feat but this book will take you through the journey to success. It will give you the skills to access your *Inner Warrior*.

The Inner Warrior is the *source* from which you derive the courage and the will to act in accordance with your values, attitudes and beliefs.

It is a philosophy of life that encompasses your vision of how you want the world to be yet that will not happen unless you act. So you must:

- Do it now!
- Be compassionate
- Be decent
- Fight for what is right
- Overturn injustice

It also includes a philosophy of how you want to be in the world – who you are, how you want to be seen and what you want to be known for.

The *Outer Warrior* or simply, Warrior, is the physical manifestation of the Inner Warrior. Whether or not you behave as a Warrior will depend on the degree to which you are connected to your Inner Warrior.

## THE SIX Cs OF THE INNER WARRIOR

The Inner Warrior relies on the *Six Cs* to bring about the world that you want to create. Much of our life is spent in institutions and organizations made up of interdependent groups of people or teams. (The term 'group' is used here to also refer to 'dyads' of two people.) As Sherwood and Hoylman (1977) put it:

> If a creature came from another planet to study earth civilization and returned to give a report, a 'fair witness' about us would be, 'They do almost everything in groups. They grow up in groups, learn in groups, play in groups, live in groups and work in groups'.

Many of these groups, at home, at school, with friends, in higher education and at work are structured around task *achievement and approval*. As a result, interpersonal and intergroup *competition* is often at large and frequently encouraged.

This emphasis on competition and tangible achievements with little or no attention to their personal and interpersonal effects, leaves many people entering groups without:

1. *Conflict:* An insight into how conflict impinges on our Inner and Outer Warrior and hence our mode of operating when friction is around.
2. *Concepts:* A conceptual framework to diagnose group process – the behaviour and dynamics of any group that works closely together.
3. *Collaboration:* An understanding of how to reduce unhealthy egocentric conflict and competition that are costly to individuals, the team and the organization and instead create a collaborative climate.
4. *Consensus:* Effective ways of retaining a controlled, forthright and receptive attitude whilst raising and working through problems and disagreements – be they interpersonal, interfunctional or related to business issues.
5. *Compassion:* The knowledge to replace habitual and ineffective responses with ones that facilitate problem-solving and commitment to agreed decisions – at both the task and interpersonal levels.
6. *Courage:* A philosophy which will help you find your voice and use the previous five Cs, whatever the circumstances, in a determined effort to change your life and work experiences.

## THE GULLIVER EFFECT

My view represents a paradigm shift in thinking as regards change. This book, far from asking how we can change people, is asking how we can prevent people from changing.

People in organizations often unconsciously behave as Gulliver did when in Lilliput. Like Gulliver, all too often in groups people feel shackled by invisible ties which they perceive they are powerless to free themselves from.

After training and development, people frequently learn that they are, in fact, free to stand up and be counted. Yet when they get back to their desks, they are reluctant to behave accordingly for fear of disrupting the group, hurting people or being hurt themselves, as was Gulliver on discovering that he could be free if he so chose.

By choosing to hold back, people allow an unhealthy situation to fester so that when they finally feel they have no option but to break free and stand up for themselves, their frustration and anger mean they do so unskilfully. This, as Gulliver found to his cost, causes precisely the disruption and hurt they sought to avoid by accommodating the bad behaviour of others.

This book will show how, by drawing on the principles of the Six Cs we can:

■ ensure that the 'honeymoon period' endures
■ design training and development that facilitates our changing back to who we were before we became 'institutionalized'

Gulliver made a decision to change his behaviour; to stand up and be the giant person he was. Had Gulliver (1) been brave enough to confront head on the *conflict* his decision would cause (2) possessed the *concepts* to understand the significance of the behaviours of group members and the effects his change would have on them (3) understood the significance of seeking *collaboration* when deciding how he implemented his change (4) been able to remain calm and in control until *consensus* was reached such that people willingly helped him carry out his decision (5) shown *compassion* to indulge those with opposing interests and viewpoints and (6) the *courage* to act on his conviction at the right time (before he became frustrated and angry) – *then* he would have achieved a win–win.

Without these skills, philosophy and concepts, we either opt out of doing what we believe is right or do it so unskilfully that we do not achieve what we set out to. Either way we fail.

Learning the skills and philosophy of the Six Cs will provide the courage to unmask and challenge those who place personal interests above those of the organization. As a result, the foundations of the barriers, both within people and without, will crumble.

By developing courage and finding their Inner Warrior, people can perform to their full potential and get the recognition they deserve; and organizations will become strong and unified, and will reward their real talent.

If at the start of this book you are:

- Conforming
- Avoiding
- Resentful
- Depressed
- Guilty
- Put upon
- Disillusioned
- Underachieving
- Used and abused
- Disconnected and directionless

Or are simply:

- Seeking to be the best you can be
- Wanting to develop yourself to the fullest
- Longing to use your potential
- Wishing to know more about change
- Keen to unleash real performance improvement in your organization

At the end of this book you will be:

- Free
- Powerful
- A Warrior prepared to fight for your rights and the rights of others
- Insisting the organization's goals are put first
- Not tolerating game playing
- Prepared to help others to do the same
- Energized by the fact that your actions are having the desired effect
- An important part of the success of the organization
- Better able to effect the changes you always knew you could make
- Equipped with more tools to successfully improve organization performance
- Achieving
- Successful
- Fulfilled

Throughout the book I use real case studies and examples where clients have achieved just such a transformation in every aspect of their lives. However, their names have been change to protect their privacy.

In organizations, for you this could mean providing an equal contribution to creative problem-solving sessions or breaking down barriers between divisional silos, or diminishing the power of the few by instigating improved teamwork on a project or finally confronting the game playing of a persistently obstructive colleague or being proactive to derive more value from an appraisal. This will enable everyone who is passionate about securing justice, effectiveness and success to learn how to do so for themselves and the organization.

BEVERLEY STONE

# Acknowledgements

This book is the culmination of many years spent working as a consultant with individuals and teams to develop their authenticity, integrity and courage when pursuing personal and organizational goals. So first and foremost, I'd like to thank the many people I have been privileged to work with for their willingness to be open and trusting while taking the risk of being themselves.

I also want to thank a number of extremely busy clients, colleagues, friends and family who were happy to spend time reading the manuscript and provide me with useful comments and perspectives: Debbie Hewitt, Rosemary Chesters, Jevan Morris, Lord Stone of Blackheath, Lulu Stone, Karen Geary and Rachel Baird.

A huge thank you to Jon Lamb for our times together creating, discussing, arguing and mostly laughing, whilst he helped me put my excited ramblings of ideas, views and passions into more logical and linear prose and format.

I must thank Stephen Rutt, my publishing editor, for his wisdom which astounds me. Once again, he allowed me to meddle with the structure of the book before returning to his original, faultless counsel. And thank you to Anna van Boxel and Ciara O'Conner for all the help with the manuscript and the marketing. Also, as someone who finds being systematic and methodical very difficult, I both admire and am profoundly grateful to the team at Aardvark Editorial for all their hard work.

The author would like to thank Marvin Dunnette, editor of *The Handbook of Industrial and Organizational Psychology*, 1976, Palo Alto, CA: Consulting Psychologists Press for permission to use and develop the Thomas–Kilmann conflict-handling model.

# PART I

# The Problem Unveiled

# CHAPTER 1

# THE INNER WARRIOR

You're sitting in the boardroom, you've got butterflies in your stomach and you feel as if you're on the edge of a precipice. You want to say something but you don't know whether you're going to fall to the bottom and crash and die or whether you're going to be an authentic person and fly. You know many in the room will agree with you because when you broke earlier for coffee they told you so. But in the room you're convinced that nobody will follow your lead or be there to save you if you fall. But, heart in mouth, you take the leap and you fly. As a result, you feel like a hero!

You are standing in front of 150 people, it will be the first presentation you've ever given. Waves of fear wash over you because you fantasize that your audience is either not interested in what you have to say or better informed on the subject than you. You are conscious that your mind is blank, your heart is racing. Now is the moment. You know you must operate from your gut, your passion for the subject and not from within your head as the delivery would then be disjointed. You tell yourself you are on your own here, it's down to you. You take a deep breath and access your Inner Warrior. As the audience looks up at you expectantly, you do not flinch, you embrace the task at hand, you are courageous. You knock 'em dead!

You're about to become a whistle-blower. You've muttered in the ranks with others for some time. One day something happens that makes you realize you can no longer endure being the person you've become; institutionalized, a shadow of yourself, living a lie. You are compelled to report what you know to your boss. Now you are in his office, waiting for him to finish the call he is making. You are nervous, perspiring. Finally, he finishes his call and replaces the receiver, his chair swings around and he looks you in the eye as if to say, 'Yes, what's so important?' The challenge in his eyes is enough. Nothing is going to stop you now. All the fears and doubts, the need to fit in, the fear of being sacked or blacklisted are irrelevant. All that matters is that you are true to yourself in doing the right thing by other people and the organization. You access your Inner Warrior. You speak. The moment your words are out in the ether, everything has changed forever. You feel good. You feel powerful. You're being the person you know yourself to be.

## VALUES – LIVED NOT LAMINATED!

The situations above are all examples of when we are being the person we would wish ourselves to be. At these 'crunch moments' we are truly authentic. We feel alive.

Although we may experience this sensation in our organizations, the reality is that for many of us it only occurs outside of work: when confronting bad customer service, fighting for our cause as a local councillor or speaking up as a school governor. At these times in life, there is complete harmony between how we see ourselves and how we are perceived by those around us. We feel highly energized, capable of doing anything with our lives. This is the person we really are.

Wouldn't it be good if we experienced our whole life in this way? Of course it would. Yet all too frequently in organizations, I find that people do not speak out at a meetings but, instead, are the ones huddled around the coffee machine talking about what should have been said. Their presentation went badly wrong because their minds went blank and they could not pull themselves out of it. Or they do not 'blow the whistle'.

What they do, rather, is regret lost opportunities. Worse still, when this happens often enough, they also regret the loss of themselves. They disappoint and confuse themselves because on these occasions their behaviour does not correspond to the way they think of themselves.

At first they feel angry with others, blaming the organization, colleagues or their boss. Then they start to feel angry with themselves. This anger, turned inward, consists of a flow of self-criticism which causes a sense of helplessness and hopelessness. Working life becomes pretty meaningless but they feel powerless to change things. Eventually, this sense of powerlessness will cause them to feel depressed (Seligman, 1974).

In organizations, I work with many clients who have given in and given up to their fate. They'll say:

- 'It's not worth it – I'll be demolished.'
- 'What's the point? Nothing will change.'
- 'It's not that bad.'

But in this way, they merely prolong the discomfort that they endure every day. They become half the person they really are. The life they should be living escapes them. They are not living up to their values.

## WHAT'S IT GOT TO DO WITH THE PRICE OF FISH?

How can so many people feel this way, given that so many organizations proclaim people are their greatest asset?

Let us assume our computer has developed a gremlin. We have a project to finish and we need access to the internet to do so. What do we do? If we do not have access to technical support we reach for a manual and attempt to solve the problem ourselves. Everything that we need to solve this problem is contained in the manual. If we follow it to the letter we will eventually find the solution.

Now let us consider there is a new impediment to achieving our project on time. It comes in the form of Thomas, an obstructive member of staff who, true to form, is withholding cooperation just when we need it most. What do we do? We think of how we might talk Thomas round and achieve cooperation. Attempts at this fail. We then decide to go to the 'manual' – texts on organizational behaviour and change. We read up on how to achieve effective cultures and interpersonal relationships at work and, utilizing this information, return to ask for Thomas's cooperation. He still doesn't give it.

Why is it that the manuals for machines will help us and those that relate to humans do not? Especially when most obstructions at work are in the form of other people. The answer is that the material available does not acknowledge the real problem. There are plenty of 'motherhood statements' that no one in their right mind would disagree with. Examples include:

| | |
|---|---|
| *Organization values:* | Listen |
| | Respect |
| | Honest |
| | Innovative |
| | Open-minded |
| *Successful change programmes:* | Create a vision |
| | Communicate the vision |
| | Empower people to act on the vision |
| | Create short-term 'wins' |

Consolidate improvements to produce
further change
Embed new approaches

*Reasons for resistance to change:*     The shock of the new
Economic implications
Security in the past
Fear of the unknown
Threats to relationships, status or skill

## MIND THE GAP

The problem is, following the handbook has little or no effect in the real
world. This is the gap between the textbook and the world as it is actually
lived. It is one of many gaps that we find in our organizations. Here are
some others:

- Gap between the course room theory and its practical application
- Gap between the workshop 'esprit de corps' and 'back at the ranch'
- Gap between the meeting culture and the coffee machine culture
- Gap between the laminated values of the leadership and those that are
  lived

These gaps exist because training and development is not focused at the
right level. I want to bridge that gap.

Theories and courses are not addressing the real problem and the real
problem lies within each and every one of us. For this reason the gap
between the actual problem and the generic solutions remains unbridged.

## THE MORE THINGS CHANGE, THE MORE THEY STAY THE SAME

We can read all the texts we like. We can attend any number of courses.
But, unless we can say for certain that when left to our own devices we are
equipped to deal with, for example, the ambush in the corridor or the
hijacking of a meeting, organizations will never effect real and lasting
change in their cultures.

When expensive and lengthy change programmes based on human
relations concepts do not deliver what they promise, consultants, HR
professionals and leaders lose faith – and patience! – and come to believe
there is a straight choice between a people-centred approach to manage-

ment and the bottom line. And they tend to choose the bottom line – by cutting costs, downsizing and so on.

But I would argue that choosing to focus on the bottom line *means* adopting a people-centred approach – the two go hand in hand. So there is no choice. I *can*, on the other hand, understand the disenchantment with the numerous change programmes designed to change the culture since:

- they take too long
- they generally make no lasting difference

They do not deliver the promised changes to the climate of the organization. So, in that sense, the more things change, the more they stay the same.

If we can find a solution that quickly and effectively addresses these human relations issues we will all win. We will have healthy people working in healthy organizations.

What organizations need is that their people can call upon the same strength that they demonstrate elsewhere in their lives to use at will within the workplace. The foundation of this strength is what I call the Inner Warrior.

---

Theoretical accounts of

organizational change and development

and

A call for values, attitudes and beliefs

in line with best practice

PLUS

Awakening the Inner Warrior:

Each individual having the courage of their convictions =

VALUES – LIVED NOT LAMINATED!

---

## THE INNER WARRIOR AND THE FOUR OUTER PERSONAS

The Inner Warrior is a potent source of our motivation, will and strength. If we connect to it, successfully, we will be filled with courage and compelled to act in accordance with our values, attitudes and beliefs.

Who has an Inner Warrior? We all do. Everyone enjoys access to their Inner Warrior and our warrior-like behaviour derives from it. As I said earlier, we all recognize times when we are connected to our Inner Warrior and fight for what is right, defend someone else or make our point heard. But equally we recognize times when we do not.

The level of skill we exhibit depends on the level of connectivity we have at the time to our inner strength and philosophy – our Inner Warrior. There are four levels of connection and therefore four types of persona:

1. *Warrior* – I'm fighting for myself and my 'tribe'
2. *Lamb* – I feel led like a lamb to the slaughter
3. *Hijacker* – We're doing things my way or not at all
4. *Shadow* – At work I'm a shadow of my former self

Our behaviour will reflect one of the above based on the following two variables:

■ How often we connect to our Inner Warrior at key moments
■ How well we use the relational skills and concepts of the Six Cs

This is illustrated in Figure 1.1.

We may well behave as any of these types during the course of our working day. This will depend on the situation we find ourselves in. However, as we become settled in our jobs, we will have a tendency to behave as one of the four types, as a result of our learnt response to stressful situations and whether we are philosophically inclined to be egocentric or altruistic. Other influencing factors include past experiences and our level of knowledge of the people and task at hand.

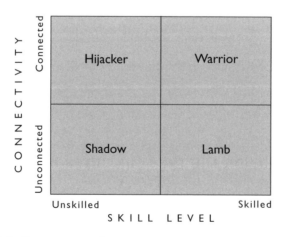

**Figure 1.1** Four types of persona

## FEARLESS: THE WARRIOR AND THE ABYSS

A key component of being a Warrior is preparedness for *risk taking*. Only once we are able to view failure as a learning experience are we ready to take those risks.

Failure can be represented as the abyss we all fear falling into. The Warrior has no qualms about staring into the abyss and stepping forward if he knows it is the right thing to do.

- *Warriors* – always jump and land gracefully
- *Lambs* – sometimes jump and land gracefully
- *Hijackers* – always jump but land clumsily
- *Shadows* – never jump

Many people in organizations appear to be standing frozen on the edge of an abyss agonizing over taking the risk of jumping. I suggest they jump! Either they'll fly or they won't but they'll never know until they take the risk and try. I do not urge people to abandon their comfortable lives, but by the time they come to see me, their comfortable lives have become intolerable.

# The Lamb

## The Lamb and the Abyss

As Lambs we behave in a warrior-like fashion sporadically. We do not fear the consequences of our actions when laying down the law as chairman of the PTA yet refrain from such warrior-like behaviour at work. We believe that if we behaved with the courage of our convictions in our organization, the consequences would be far more serious. We live with the 'catastrophic fantasies' – catastrophic because we always think the worst, fantasies because the worst rarely happens – that if we spoke up we might be ostracized by leaders or colleagues.

When behaving as a Lamb, what we perceive to be at stake is affecting our ability to be a Warrior. We are standing at the precipice looking into the abyss and we don't like what we see. There's no way we are going to jump.

## Connectivity – Sporadic

> I can't understand myself. On occasion I find it easy to argue with someone who is being difficult, I'm prepared to stand my ground no matter what. But most of the time I could kick myself because I know what we're doing is wrong but I say nothing. I feel totally paralysed.
>
> *Susie Chambers, IT consultant*

When we are behaving as Lambs we are unconsciously competent because there are times in our lives when we can access our Inner Warrior quite readily and there are other times when we feel powerless to do so. So, as Lambs, although at times we act as Warriors, mostly we are not being true to ourselves. And we have very little understanding of what differentiates the two situations.

## Philosophy – Altruistic

At work, by caring for other people's feelings and being almost too altruistic, we are completely incapable of asserting ourselves. Or it may be that within our organizations we can assert ourselves in one situation but not in another. The result is that we become frustrated with ourselves for this lack of consistency in standing up for what we believe in. And consequently, the organization suffers because it is not reaping the benefits of our integrity and potential.

## Relational Skills

As Lambs we have generally good interpersonal skills until stressed by, say, the threat of conflict and disagreements, when our response will be to passively *accommodate*.

| *Typically* | *Stress response* |
|---|---|
| ▪ Supportive | ▪ Conforming |
| ▪ Respectful | ▪ Self-sacrificing |
| ▪ Willing | ▪ Pliable |
| ▪ Dependable | ▪ Dependent |
| ▪ Agreeable | ▪ Submissive |

## Characteristics

Here is what some people have said about their behaviour as Lambs:

- *Inauthentic:* 'I'm sitting there knowing what I could be like and yet feel so tongue-tied. Why can't I find my voice, I scream silently to myself.' We can play out what we want to happen over and over in our head but we cannot cross the Rubicon and make it happen. We have a good, healthy self-image but lack the courage to bring about what we believe is right.

- *Unfulfilled and regretful:* 'How much longer can I live like this? I'm wasting my life. When is my turn? It keeps me awake at night. I go over conversations in which I regret not having said something. Or else

I rehearse conversations I'm going to have in the future. Yet when it comes to the crunch I lose my nerve.' 'I know I'm worth more than others currently believe but, because it remains hidden, I'm not treated as I think I should be.' As Lambs more than any type, we are plagued with regret. We are waiting for someone else to give us a turn but since nobody does, we remain sitting in the waiting room of life.

■ *Suppressed creativity:* 'I sit thinking, I can't believe we've sat here for an hour going round and round in circles when there's an obvious answer.' As Lambs we are a bundle of ideas; ideas about how we could make improvements to our job, our teamwork, and our organizations, but we don't always have the courage to tell anyone.

■ *Overconsiderate:* 'I'm constantly putting everyone's needs first, hoping that others will do the same for me. When they don't, I feel let-down and hurt, yet continue to give – and give in!' 'Well, I mean I like to do the right thing, I don't want to make waves and it isn't that much skin off my nose really is it? My boss is very good to me, all things considered so I'm sure there's a reason why he's moved me across into that job. As long as I stay on the right side of people, I can sleep at night.' In the most extreme cases we are, in effect, waiting for 'the grown ups' to give us permission to join them.

■ *Anxious:* 'I get so frustrated with myself. I feel an anxiety in my gut that I don't feel anywhere but at work. All the times it's really important for me to speak out, I'm scared to.' Being left behind, left out and misperceived eventually takes its toll.

## The Shadow

### The Shadow and the Abyss

Inside, as Shadows, we long to be seen as the person we know we could be. There is a nagging feeling in our souls that there must be more to life. At some level we possess an inner drive towards self-fulfilment but do not have an image of what we are growing from or to. We only know that the way we are seen and treated is incongruent with something buried deep within us.

So we sit in meetings, detached from the group, pretending not to see the lies and the deceit rather than take the risk of jumping into the abyss and remaining true to ourselves.

## Connectivity – Limited

> I'm damned if I'm going to use any more energy on that lot in there. I just sit and do what's asked of me. Of course, there's a limit to how much anyone can take. I get my own back in subtle ways…
>
> *Joe Kemp, civil servant*

As Shadows we have never really developed our Inner Warrior – a strong sense of who we are and what we want – and therefore find it difficult, if not impossible, to access it without help. We feel unfulfilled in life but do not know what would fulfil us. We may connect to our Inner Warrior, with a little Dutch courage, but not so much that it impacts on our lives.

## Philosophy – Initially Altruistic Becoming Egocentric

In the organization Shadow people will be reliable, loyal and meticulous. However, if they feel put-upon, the organization will never get more from them than precisely what it asks for – and in this day and age, that is no longer enough. We cannot afford to have people walking around as 'empty shells' if we are to find a competitive edge. Nor can any organization that professes to care about work–life balance tolerate this type of condition among its people. Put simply, neither the organization nor the individual can remain healthy in this state.

## Relational Skills

When behaving as Shadows we display poor people skills. Our *response* to stressful situations – those in which we find our ego is threatened – will be *avoidance* which at best will mean opting out and at worst, resorting to passive–aggressive revenge cycles. Passive–aggressive behaviour refers to covert obstructionism, procrastination, stubbornness or deliberate ineffi-ciency. Such behaviour is a manifestation of passively expressed, under-lying aggression.

| *Typically* | *Stress response* |
|---|---|
| ▪ Industrious | ▪ Unsympathetic |
| ▪ Diplomatic | ▪ Unresponsive |
| ▪ Serious | ▪ Unhelpful |
| ▪ Persistent | ▪ Moralistic |
| ▪ Exacting | ▪ Manipulative |

## Characteristics

Here is what some of these people have said:

(a) *Cowed:* 'I have to do what the boss says. You break the rules and you're in deep trouble.' If our general stance is that of the Shadow we will have issues with authority. We may begin by being in awe of those in authority and put them on a pedestal. We then either sense-lessly despise them or unquestioningly admire them. If, as Shadows, we despise authority, we become passive–aggressive. If we admire them we become blindly obedient.

(b) *Misperceived:* 'If people knew me as I really am they would treat me differently. They would listen to me more and have more respect for my opinions and contributions.'

(c) *Detached:* 'I just think I'm damned if I'm going to get into another argument with that aggressive, self-promoting fool. I say to myself, I know you, you know I've got your number and that's enough for me right now, but just you wait.' This is an example of passive–aggres-sive behaviour. As Shadows, we are overly concerned with the opin-ions of others and usually assume they are negative. To protect ourselves against the fear of rejection, we reject first.

(d) *Invisible:* 'I'm saying to myself, I really don't agree with you but is it really worth arguing about?' As Shadows, we are continually over-looked – overlooked for promotion, reward, extra responsibility – and we feel invisible as a result.

(e) *Low-energy:* As Shadows we can appear robotic and show little or no passion for anything since we are not connected to our gut, our soul, and our Inner Warrior.

# The Hijacker

## The Hijacker and the Abyss

When roused, as Hijackers we have no interest in the other people in the room. We are totally driven by our ego. The situation is a personal one, a battle to be won, and we are going to win! More than happy to jump into the abyss, we continue to restate our position saying it louder and more slowly, making the other person feel stupid and inadequate. We hijack the meeting. We hope that the sheer unwavering stance we hold will help us get our way eventually. It does, but only for a short time – until the meeting ends!

Although as Hijackers, we use logic and reason to justify our argument, others can see we are coming from a different place entirely. We intend to get our own way and do not see that this has been achieved at the expense of real as opposed to 'apparent' agreement – and hence a lack of real commitment.

## Connectivity – Fully

> Look, I am not prepared to sit here and wait for people to do things in their own time, in their own way. If they can't keep up with me, that's their tough luck. Half the people in here should be sacked anyway, they're totally unprofessional and incompetent.
>
> *Rosemary Visozo, IT manager*

As Hijackers we have a consistent connection to our Inner Warrior but will use this connection to stand up for ourselves with little regard for others. Our behaviours will not, therefore, ultimately bring benefit to ourselves or anyone else.

## Philosophy – Egocentric

As Hijackers we tend to hold beliefs and values that are at odds with those of our organization. Whereas it is likely that an organization will have humanistic assumptions about human behaviour which maintain that, given the right encouragement, people will naturally work hard and creatively to achieve and self-actualize, Hijackers will hold values which are more autocratic assuming other people (not themselves) are naturally lazy and need to be monitored and controlled. This will result in their creating a fear culture, where those not used to accessing their Inner Warrior will sublimate it to an aggressive stance.

If there are enough Hijackers in power in an organization they can even subdue the Warrior, who will either opt out of the organization psychologically or leave physically.

## Relational Skills

As Hijackers we have excellent people skills until stressed, when our *response* to stress will be *autocratic,* sometimes combining an aggressive outburst.

| *Typically* | *Stress response* |
| --- | --- |
| ▪ Strong willed | ▪ Bombastic |
| ▪ Independent | ▪ Argumentative |

- Practical
- Decisive
- Efficient

- Critical
- Dominating
- Unyielding

## Characteristics

Here is what some of these people have said:

(a) *Emotion overtaking reason:* 'I can't believe that these people can't see what I'm saying. I feel as though I have to repeat it four times in four different ways even though it's obvious and logical.'

(b) *Self-justification:* 'I'm the only sane person in the room!' 'I'm not here to worry about your feelings – just to get the job done.' When being a Hijacker we are clumsy, not skilful. This is because we have little or no awareness of the impact of our style. When in a facilitated discussion, for example, and receiving feedback, we are genuinely shocked that we are seen as rude, insensitive or aggressive by other team members.

(c) *Lack of respect:* 'You people are utterly incompetent. There is simply no way this should have been allowed to happen. Well it has – and I hold you personally responsible.' As Hijackers, we believe that we can use the sheer force of our argument to bludgeon our way to victory. We make others feel that there is no middle ground – either they agree with us and see things our way, or they are fools for disagreeing.

(d) *Alive:* 'I was revelling in the fact that I was right. I feel great, emotions coursing through me – I feel alive and powerful.' Even if we know we cannot win, we get a 'kick' out of going down fighting.

(e) *Ego-overdrive!* 'It felt good to get that off my chest.' As Hijackers, we feel giddy with our own anger. We're on our own, but unlike the Warrior who is a lone star fighting for their philosophy, at these times, we are a lone wolf fighting for our ego.

# The Warrior

### The Warrior and the Abyss

As Warriors, we are too busy following our hearts to see the abyss, let alone wonder whether or not to jump. But on the rare occasions when we do see an abyss, it does not take long for us to summon up the courage to jump. As Warriors, we do not really see that there is a choice. Maintaining our integrity is valued far more highly than the alternative of succumbing to seeking the approval of others, or the false hope that someone else will do the right thing on our behalf.

On the rare occasions that we do not jump, we quickly learn from our feelings of guilt and either go back and redress the balance or, if this is not possible, ensure that the same thing never happens again.

## Connectivity – Fully

> I don't understand why people stand around and moan about what is and isn't happening in the organization. If they feel so strongly about it why don't they say something? I'll tell you one thing I wouldn't hang around in an organization that didn't value me, I'd either speak up or ship out!
>
> *David Burns, sales executive*

As Warriors, we have unceasing access to our Inner Warrior – it is a part of our make-up. Warriors are the people we admire for standing up in a company meeting and speaking out on behalf of the silent majority. In an AGM they are the director who doesn't fob off a difficult questioner but rather empathizes and tries to clarify the problem and seek a solution. They exude an air of confidence, such as that of President Clinton, Margaret Thatcher or Richard Branson.

## Philosophy – Altruistic

Such Warriors are like a beacon of integrity that stands out against the cold, self-serving approach of many representatives of our organizations. It is the activities of such people that provide the ethical bedrock of our organizational strategy. Such people are prepared to take risks, to act when they can no longer stay silent. We not only need to value and encourage these people as role models, we need them to develop and inspire other role models. Without such people, who are prepared to take the risk to live the stated values, who knows in which direction our companies will go?

## Relational Skills – Excellent

As Warriors, we have excellent people skills generally, and our *response* in stressful situations such as speaking up in meetings, giving a presentation or whistle-blowing, will be to *initiate* a collaborative dialogue in an attempt to solve the problem.

| *Typically* | *Stress response* |
|---|---|
| ■ Exploring | ■ Confrontational |
| ■ Stimulating | ■ Excitable |
| ■ Enthusiastic | ■ Disciplined |
| ■ Dramatic | ■ Proactive |
| ■ Friendly | ■ Passionate |

## Characteristics

The characteristics of the Warrior can best be summed up by what some people have said:

(a) *Passionate and powerful yet calm:* 'Because I work from an altruistic philosophy, I have a sense that everybody feels the same as I do – so I do what I do on their behalf. It feels powerful!'

(b) *Separate:* 'By being separate, knowing everyone is frozen by my courage, yet willing me on, I am energized.' 'Nobody's going to support what I'm saying and nobody's going to rescue me if I get into trouble – but that won't stop me saying what I believe.'

(c) *Excited and motivated:* 'I feel excited and motivated because I'm following my philosophy – I'm doing it now. I'm going be a hero! My philosophy is to unmask any deception, games or manipulation. My integrity won't allow me to let this pass by. I will not allow myself to live in an unreal world where the power is in the hands of self-serving individuals.'

(d) *Elevated:* 'I try and be the bigger person.' When we behave like a Warrior, we elevate a level and become the statesman.

(e) *Charismatic:* One of the characteristics of a being a Warrior is that we are charismatic. You may be thinking that Hitler, Stalin, and Saddam Hussein were charismatic. Weren't they Warriors? Yes, they were, they were charismatic, passionate, separate, excited and motivated. The point is that, to be a Warrior we use collaboration, compassion and consensus and the others of the Six Cs. Without these skills and knowledge we attempt to influence by demolishing other people's arguments and are, instead, a Hijacker masquerading as a Warrior, as were the three leaders mentioned above.

These four types are summarized in Table 1.1.

| **Table 1.1** Characteristics of the four types | | | | |
|---|---|---|---|---|
| | **LAMB** | **SHADOW** | **HIJACKER** | **WARRIOR** |
| Connectivity to our Inner Warrior | Sporadic | Limited | Full | Full |
| Philosophy | Altruistic | Altruistic/ egocentric | Egocentric | Altruistic |
| Stress response | Accommodate | Avoid | Autocratic | Initiate |
| Characteristics | Inauthentic<br><br>Unfulfilled and regretful<br>Suppressed creativity<br>Overconsiderate<br>Anxious<br>Fearful | Cowed<br><br>Misperceived<br>Detached<br>Invisible<br>Low energy<br>Fearful | Emotion overtakes reason<br>Self-justification<br>Lack of respect<br>Alive<br>Ego-overdrive<br>Fearless | Passionate, power- ful yet calm<br>Separate<br>Excited & motivated<br>Elevated<br>Charismatic<br>Fearless |
| Outcomes | Periodically effective | Ineffective | Short term Effective | Effective |

## OVERVIEW AND CONCLUSION

Depending on how connected we are to our Inner Warrior, we will behave as one of the following four types:

1. As a *Lamb*, we will comply with the views and requests of others whilst withholding our own. The loss to the organization and to our own lives is clear.
2. As a *Shadow*, we will be present in body but not in spirit. By neither openly supporting the views and requests of our colleagues, nor voicing our own we are clearly a liability to everyone including ourselves.
3. As a *Hijacker*, we will forcefully voice our opinions and even achieve apparent agreement in the short term whilst people are in our company. However, our lack of influencing skills will not inspire long-term loyalty or commitment to any decision made.
4. As a *Warrior*, we possess not only the courage to speak our minds and the skills to encourage others to do so, but also the ability to inspire commitment to agreed decisions.

Imagine how productive team meetings and one-to-one conversations would be if we were all to awaken our Inner Warrior and behave as Warriors – being the person we know ourselves to be – not only in our family and social groups but also in our working groups too.

# CHAPTER 2

# THE GULLIVER EFFECT

## THE QUESTION OF CHANGE REFRAMED

We constantly say that we want to use the talents of everyone in our organizations. From organization-wide change programmes to individual mentoring and coaching, we do our utmost to make it a reality.

Isn't it frustrating, then, that no matter how much time and money is spent, we often see little overall rewards for our efforts? We may see one or two 'stars' who have really benefited from their experiences, but in general the culture remains more or less the same. How can this be when, at the close of many development workshops, people appear to leave with a real 'buzz' of team spirit, insight and good intentions. How come this dissipates almost as soon as they get back to their desks?

(a) Some say it is because people are incapable of change (for example Adrian Furnham, 2003)
(b) Some because the way change is implemented results in their resistance to it (Hussey, 1998)
(c) Others imply resistance to change is inevitable and needs specific remedies (Kotter et al., 1986).

My view is that, far from asking how we can change our people, we should instead be asking – How can we *prevent* them from changing?

Why? Because the reality is, merely as a result of working in a hierarchical, structured organization, our people have become 'institutionalized'. Within weeks or months of joining, people undergo significant personal change, whether we instigate it or not.

Consider this: we take on a new member of staff for whom we have high hopes and observe them change from:

1. The initial interview where we are so impressed because they are interesting and interested.
2. To the 3- to 6-month *honeymoon period*, which justifies our decision, and during which they are working with vigour, enthusiasm and innovation.
3. To the post-honeymoon period, when they are now either:
   - sitting silently in meetings and later whispering in corridors, or
   - struggling to remain a 'hero' in the face of uncooperative colleagues, or
   - bulldozing their way through opposition in pursuit of personal agendas.

   It should be clear then that people can and do change!

Therefore, if we want to get the most out of our people the first step is to:

- diagnose the problem correctly, and then
- initiate the correct solution.

I suggest that we seriously consider the term *honeymoon period* in relation to both the diagnosis and the solution. The honeymoon period denotes the time when, because we are new to the business, we are given leave to think creatively, suggest and implement new ideas, and ask for and receive resources and information. This period is generally being watched by colleagues with a mixture of admiration, friendliness and jealousy. Soon the jealousy overwhelms the admiration and friendliness and we begin to experience resistance. Implicit cultural norms – unspoken terms of engagement – are now being brought to bear and slowly learnt. We begin to sense whose toes not to tread on, when to ask for permission, how to offer suggestions, not to act autonomously nor ask for more resources and so on. Our honeymoon period is over. We begin to become one of the crowd – a bona fide member of the institutionalized group.

If we recognize that our problem is that many people change – usually for the worse – soon after joining the business, the solution is far less daunting. Helping people acquire the courage to remain themselves or to return to their old selves is easier than – unnecessarily – compelling them to unlearn habits of a lifetime and replace them with new ones. If the change that results from being institutionalized is anticipated and addressed, we might well find that resistance to the type of change we want to effect through change programmes is no longer inevitable.

## THE GULLIVER EFFECT

My experience of working in many organizations tells me that people have changed so much they can no longer recognize themselves. They may not openly show it but many lose self-confidence, suffer nagging doubts and feel less themselves. It is this that they tell me bothers them. And it is this that should be bothering senior executives and HR professionals. This is what I call the Gulliver Effect.

Within each of us we have the power of a giant when we're operating at full capacity. But if we are in a typical politicized environment then we will suffer the same fate as Gulliver.

During his seafaring expeditions, Jonathan Swift's Gulliver is shipwrecked on an island called Lilliput. Tired and exhausted, he sleeps soundly through the night only to awake to find he is a prisoner of the island's tiny inhabitants.

- *Phase one:* The Lilliputians have used many pieces of string to secure him to the ground. He assumes he's a captive.

- *Phase two:* He manages to free an arm and loosen the ties on his head, but his captors fire hundreds of tiny arrows wounding him enough to deter him from any further attempt to escape.

- *Phase three:* He knows he has the power to break free, stand up and be the 'giant' he is on this island. But he decides to lie still and free himself at night.

  Eventually his captors establish a relationship with Gulliver, albeit one that is communicated in a language he does not understand. When he signals to them he is desperately hungry, they respond positively and bring him food and drink.

- *Phase four:* He is tempted to attack his captors, but is dissuaded from so doing by:
  1. the pain of the arrows which are lodged in his skin
  2. a sense of honour to the Lilliputians because of the generosity they have shown him.

- *Phase five:* Gulliver decides to cooperate with his captors. He accommodates them in an unhealthy agreement, avoiding conflict and making compromises. His prone state may be in the interest of the Lilliputians and their homes nearby, but it is not in his own. Even though he makes concessions he does not receive in return the behaviour he expects and deserves. Instead, his captors take advantage of his goodwill.

- *Phase six:* Finally he can take no more. Roused to anger he breaks free of the ropes, ranting and raving at his tormentors, who flee, frightened for their lives. He decides to break free in an unskilful and obvious way, rather than his first idea which was to do it secretly in the dead of night.

- *Phase seven:* Neither course was good for the group.

What did Gulliver do wrong? He should not have second-guessed the outcome and accommodated in order to (a) avoid being hurt and (b) avoiding hurting others. By not standing up to make the changes when he needed to, Gulliver broke free unskilfully and caused precisely that which he sought to avoid – disruption and hurt.

He should not have swapped one unhealthy situation for another; he does not need to apologize for who he is. His message from the start should have been – 'You need not fear me. I want what is best for *all* of us. I will not bend and compromise where there is injustice (as a Lamb or Shadow) nor will I dominate and intimidate (as a Hijacker). I will confront this situation in a calm, rational and controlled manner (as Warrior).'

The Gulliver Effect occurs when we feel we cannot stand up and be counted for fear of hurting others or ourselves. We feel imprisoned by those around us who seek to prevent us from achieving our potential and giving our all to the organization. In doing so we construct our own negative mind-map.

The Gulliver Effect occurs when:

(a) day after day, we tolerate what we know to be wrong because we make false assumptions about our rights, the rights of others and the probable outcomes of our standing up for what we believe in.
(b) after some personal development that encourages us to have the courage of our convictions, we cause offence, confusion and resistance because we do not negotiate the changes in our behaviour.

By overaccommodating, we invariably feed the ego in others. When we do finally cry 'Enough!' we do so in such a way that we are compromised and the effect is self-destructive or destructive to others.

The irony of the story of Gulliver was that he felt big and wished he were smaller. In the real world, we feel small and wish we were bigger.

## GULLIVER'S EQUIVALENT IN THE WORKPLACE

Peter Milligan is a relatively new manager who is in his post-honeymoon period. He is attending another management team meeting. Everyone around the table has developed their own way of operating within the team. Peter, though once a participating engaged person, has become a morose figure who is saying progressively little. Why? Because other team members have exploited his trusting nature to advance their own cause. He has given in to certain demanding members yet has seen no reciprocal behaviour extended to him when he tries to put forth his own.

So the change has occurred. He began as a Warrior, engaged and giving of his all and the organization stood to get the best out of him. Then, he accommodated in the face of competitive colleagues who had the potential to harm him and became a Lamb. Today, Peter's frustration spills over when he attacks his peers, his boss and the organization. Peter has finally becomes an aggressor himself – an unskilful Hijacker.

The reason is that the meeting room is Peter's Lilliput – human groups are a foreign country with people whose motives and methods of relating are the 'language' he knows little about. By trying to accommodate them and be a square peg in a round hole, he eventually gets bent out of shape. His talents are already being lost to himself and to the company. Peter has become institutionalized. He is now demotivated, unconstructive and uncooperative.

## COURAGE IN CONFLICT

The Gulliver Effect is principally caused by the threat of potentially unpleasant conflict. We avoid making waves with difficult colleagues for fear of creating an uncomfortable atmosphere that makes thing worse rather than better. When I ask clients who are the difficult people in their lives their lists include:

- The mother-in-law
- Adolescent kids
- The boss

But, our mother-in-law is not difficult when she approves of our lifestyle and fits in around us and our children. And teenagers are not difficult when they abide by rules such as not staying out beyond a reasonable hour. And a boss is not difficult if, when we request a salary increase, promotion, or a move, it is accepted as a great idea.

So when we speak of difficult people or situations we are referring to conflict scenarios. If Gulliver had thought that a request to stand up would have been granted by the Lilliputians, he would have made it right away. It was his fear of conflict that made him avoid making the request.

## OUTCOMES OF THE GULLIVER EFFECT

Anticipating non-cooperation and conflict creates anxiety and we each respond in different ways. When disconcerting group processes weave threads over our Inner Warrior, it is imprisoned and can't be released. People feel inhibited so that they find it impossible simply to be themselves – and behave instead like Lambs or Shadows. Or else they attempt to break free from these perceived threads in an unskilful and heavy-handed manner – and behave like Hijackers. Table 2.1 illustates some of the ways the Gulliver Effect is manifested in individuals, groups and organizations. In not living by those healthy values that we share with the organization, we leave the field wide open for those with warped agendas to take over and the culture remains one of:

- *Intimidation in groups or one-to-one encounters* – Individuals do not raise the real issues, but rather allow those with personal agendas to successfully pursue them.
- *Decisions made by vocal minority* – A vocal minority creates the impression that widespread support exists for their idea. Because other members fail to offer objections, the idea is accepted.

| Table 2.1  Outcomes of the Gulliver Effect | | |
|---|---|---|
| **Individual Behaviour** | **Team Behaviour** | **Organization** |
| *Fight*<br>■ we become irritable<br>■ we shout and use sarcasm<br>■ we argue for the sake of it<br>■ we are uncooperative<br>■ we block good ideas<br>■ we become self-righteous<br>■ we feel angry and resentful | ■ we sulk<br>■ we collaborate and communicate with certain people and avoid others<br>■ we talk behind people's backs and are aggressive<br>■ we say one thing and do another<br>■ we sabotage task achievement | ■ we keep our heads down and do the minimum required<br>■ we fight for what we believe in but are sabotaged nonetheless<br>■ we develop a silo-mentality<br>■ we refuse to cooperate with other functions, businesses, countries |
| *Flight*<br>■ we comply<br>■ we adopt an ultra low profile<br>■ we defer decisions<br>■ we make poor decisions<br>■ we go 'off sick'<br>■ we experience symptoms of illness<br>■ we feel incessantly tired<br>■ we resort to alcohol and drugs<br>■ we feel neglected and depressed | ■ we refuse to be a team player<br>■ we are obstructive<br>■ we absent ourselves<br>■ we avoid people, work, the building<br>■ we do our best at all times but become increasingly exhausted and demoralized<br>■ we don't commit to decisions<br>■ we carry out decisions idiosyncratically | ■ we encourage others to be similarly uncooperative<br>■ we are more loyal to customers than to our organization and colleagues<br>■ we neglect to respond to emails or other communications<br>■ we expend energy on the lookout for a job elsewhere<br>■ we lose enthusiasm and motivation for the vision<br>■ we resist change! |

■ *Corridor meetings* – In the safety of subgroups of like-minded colleagues, friends and family, real feelings and opinions are expressed explosively and with incredulity.

Rather than assert our own opinion, we instead say little in the belief that it is easier to accommodate, avoid or compromise. In other words, we find ourselves spending much of our working life in the bottom triangle of Figure 2.1. This model, and its significance in group dynamics and interpersonal relationships, is developed in Chapter 7, 'Conflict', the first of the Six Cs.

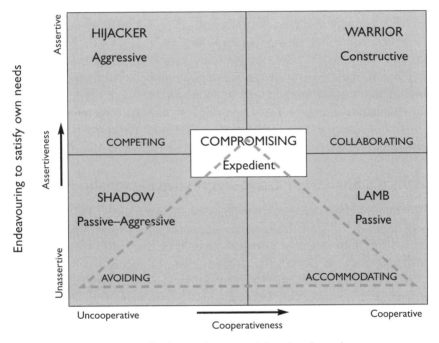

**Figure 2.1** Modes of coping with conflict

*Source:* Adapted from Thomas and Kilmann, 1974

## BEWARE HABITUAL SHADOWS!

By spending our time in the bottom triangle, we all behave uncooperatively as Shadows at times, maybe stubbornly resisting cooperating just to protect ourselves and get along as best we can. And we may sometimes behave as a Hijacker and uncooperatively snap back at someone. But though our behaviour belies it, we still have good intentions. Indeed, the reason we mostly accommodate, avoid and compromise is that we are trying to do the best we can by our colleagues and companies. We are trying to be reasonable and show compassion. Our problem is simply that we confuse being reasonable and compassionate with being a doormat.

I therefore want here to make a distinction between those of us who at times resort to the behaviour of a Hijacker or Shadow and those who habitually behave that way. The major culprits of the Gulliver Effect are *habitual passive–aggressive* Shadows and *habitual aggressive* Hijackers. These are the people who create the culture of intimidation and non-cooperation which eventually results in our unassertively giving up or giving in.

Whereas habitual aggressive Hijackers are easy to spot, being openly argumentative as they are, the habitual passive–aggressive Shadow may not be. We may experience the inevitable interpersonal conflict and frustration that result from their tactics but are unable to put our finger on how they maintain their power and control. It is important therefore to understand this passive–aggressive personality and its corrosive effect on ourselves and our organizations.

## Habitual Shadows: Passive–aggressive Personalities

Habitual Shadows have passive–aggressive personalities. Passive–aggressive behaviour is the deliberate and indirect way of expressing anger. They have a very thin veneer of resentful compliance that masks their aggression towards others and their dislike of themselves. Disinclined as they are to do as others wish, they are most likely to express the opposite of the appropriate behaviour in any situation. Passive–aggressive behaviour involves manipulative schemes aimed at getting even or punishing someone. Habitual Shadows can skilfully avoid work and responsibility and be more destructive than their Hijacker colleagues who are overtly disruptive.

### Telltale signs

Some of the warning signs of passive aggression are when people:

1. resist adequate performance through stubbornness, forgetfulness, lateness, deliberate inefficiency and procrastination
2. actively obstruct others by failing to do their share
3. stall, make excuses, complain and oppose
4. feel cheated, unappreciated and misunderstood
5. blame their failures or difficulties on others

6. justify their behaviour with lofty motives, as a cover for malicious intent
7. are sullen, impatient, argumentative, cynical, sceptical and easily frustrated
8. combine passive resistance with grumbling compliance
9. are reluctant and uncooperative
10. follow orders with chronic veiled hostility and smouldering resentment

## Issues with authority

Habitual Shadows see authority as intrusive, demanding, interfering, controlling and dominating. They experience control as intolerable and have to do things their way. They will not be subject to the rules of others. These individuals also envy and resent colleagues who are viewed positively by authority. On the other hand, they also see authority as capable of giving approval and care. A key issue for them is balancing their desire to get benefits from authority figures whilst exerting their freedom and autonomy.

## Root causes

Developed in unending power struggles with parents and siblings, the passive–aggressive personality has certain beliefs about effective conflict handling.

1. They believe that dealing with disagreements behind the scenes works better than communicating openly and honestly.

2. They believe that they should be the ones who are well behaved and get along with everyone and find it difficult, therefore, to balance a business need to openly express what they really think with the need to maintain team harmony.

3. Because they were not encouraged to handle conflict during their upbringing, they lack the skills to collaboratively express disagreement and therefore believe that handling disagreement subversively is a safe route to obtaining what they want.

## Main coping strategies

Habitual Shadows use three main strategies to defend themselves:

1. *Displacement:* their main defence mechanism, they shift their anger away from more powerful targets onto those who are less able to retal-

iate or reject them. This leaves colleagues dealing with subtle sabotage the likes of which many leaders are unaware.

2. *Externalization:* they externalize their shortcomings. They deny awareness of their own provocative behaviour and the serious nature of the consequences. They do not see themselves as having a problem so that appeals to enlist cooperation are met by their blaming others.

3. *Opposition:* they strengthen their autonomy through devious opposition to authority figures. While overtly seeking favour from them, they keep their rebellion covert enough to maintain a sense of safety and allow themselves to deny malicious intent.

## Consequences

Being unpredictable produces certain rewards for the passive–aggressive Shadow. They control others by forcing them into an uncomfortable position where they are perpetually waiting for the next struggle. Relating to people with passive–aggressive personalities becomes a tense, exasperating experience where caution must be taken to avoid precipitating another incident. This leads people to minimize contact with them out of self-protection. If they sense this growing animosity they become even more aggrieved without any sense that their behaviour has contributed to the situation. The consequences of allowing Habitual Shadows to thrive can be devastating to the business. It results in poor decision making and a toxic atmosphere – leaving people unsure where others stand. And by undermining people's power and control, it eventually leads to disaffection and stress.

Habitual Shadows thrive in a work setting where there are few consequences to non-productive behaviour and few rewards for conforming to company values or where rewards are distributed arbitrarily.

## OVERVIEW AND CONCLUSION

Within any organization there is both a subversive or vocal minority – the habitual Shadows and Hijackers – who are resistant to change; and a silent majority who do not stand up to them. This is because the effect the Habitual Shadows and Hijackers have on the organization is to create widespread apprehension. I argue that, for any change programme to stand a chance of success, we must help those who are apprehensive to return to their former selves.

Individuals need to learn about:

1. Their own and others' behaviour – Hijackers, Lambs, Shadows or Warriors.
2. Their impact on others and the team dynamics – the Gulliver Effect.
3. The resultant tone of discussions and subsequent commitment to decisions.
4. The manner in which these decisions are implemented.
5. The subsequent success or failure of the team, division or business.
6. The knock-on effect on the organization's culture.

I will consider the significance of focusing on the individual in Chapter 3.

# CHAPTER 3

# DEVELOPING INDIVIDUALS: THE SIX Cs

## WINNERS AND LOSERS

I have emphasized the importance of the individual in driving organizational success. As Derek Rollinson (2002) puts it:

> Since individual performance dovetails into the performance of a group and this feeds into the performance of a whole organization, individual characteristics can have an impact on goal achievement and hence organizational effectiveness.

■ Individual > Groups > Organization

And vice versa. When the leadership makes any decision, it is people lower down the organization who actually determine whether the decision truly works. So the decisions dovetail into group performance, which will have an impact on the performance of the individual and hence organizational effectiveness.

■ Organization > Groups > Individual

Organizational success will never be truly achieved until we draw upon everyone's talent and their will to use it. I have also made the point that discovering how to coax individuals to change or to overcome resistance to change is a red herring – they already have changed. One of the key reasons for the changes taking place in them is the culture of conflict created by political activity in the organization.

When we are working collaboratively with others in our organizations we feel a great sense of satisfaction and fulfilment. We enjoy the sense of everyone feeling a winner. Winners will develop positive attitudes towards the organization, even to the extent of ignoring less favourable aspects of it.

## CUSTOMER-FIRST VERSUS 'DOG IN THE MANGER' MENTALITY

Unfortunately, whilst some of those we work with actively help us achieve our aims and objectives, other more politically inclined characters appear to go out of their way to obstruct us. Those who are blocked consistently will eventually feel like losers within the organizational setting. The most well-intentioned people will then develop cynicism, disaffection or disinterest, even towards the favourable aspects of their organization or an impending change.

This is a tremendous spur to political activity on *their* part, as they manoeuvre to retain what power they have, or acquire the levels of power they desire. Here are two examples:

1. *NHS Reforms*
When the government set out its plans for the new foundation hospitals there was resistance within the NHS, supposedly based on rational argument. But the real reason for this opposition was likely to be a disgruntlement amongst the staff at the time of proposing the change. The nurses feel they are neither appreciated nor paid sufficiently. Doctors feel under-resourced and overworked and both groups feel they are unnecessarily outnumbered by the administration and management.

So for these reasons, they no longer respond to any change with the goodwill they may well have had as idealistic students and interns at the outset of their careers.

If you listen to interviews with teachers, unions, fire-fighters, social workers, police and so forth, it frequently appears that they justify ego-driven decisions with rational explanations. Because they feel unfairly treated, they get to the point where they choose to defend their egos by being unreasonable rather than live their values and do the right thing.

Only this morning (Tuesday, February 4th 2004 Radio 4 *Today* programme), John Humphreys was reporting on the assertion of Dr Brian Jones (a now retired, former leading expert on weapons of mass destruction in the Ministry of Defence) that his views were not reflected in Downing Street's dossier on Saddam Hussein's chemical and biological capacity. John Humphreys questioned whether this was a legitimate complaint or whether Dr Brian Jones was in reality simply being a 'dog in the manger' because he felt disgruntled that his opinions had not been taken into account by his superiors.

2. *Putin and Khodorkovsky*
When Russian president Vladimir Putin ordered the arrest of the country's richest businessman he did so on the basis of fraud and tax evasion.

However, there was a widespread belief among ordinary Russians that the move was politically motivated. Observers suggested that as soon as Mikhail Khodorkovsky's political power base grew threatening, Putin found a reason to restrict the man's freedom, even though he was originally elected on the promise that he would expand democracy in Russia.

Playing politics satisfies people's needs for power and feeds their ego at the expense of participating in rational, collaborative problem solving and decision making. As such it is very rarely a means of achieving solutions that benefit the many, rather than the few.

When people have a choice between a rational decision (democracy is a good thing for Russia's development) and their ego (Khodorkovsky's power is diminishing mine), they always choose their ego!

I recently watched a TV programme about Sir Alf Ramsey and how, when he became manager of the England football team, he rubbed the FA chairman up the wrong way. The chairman's hands were tied whilst the England team and Sir Alf were successful, but the moment the team's performance diminished, the chairman's casting vote meant that Sir Alf was given notice to leave.

To replace egocentric politicking with altruistic rationality requires the determination of those who are aware of the underlying agendas to summon the courage to challenge the political individuals concerned. Sadly, while some individuals fearing the possibility of losing become Hijackers themselves, openly resisting anything that opposes their agenda, Warriors who once openly fought these bids for power, eventually become well-meaning, hardworking but frustrated Lambs and Shadows.

The following shows how an atmosphere of conflict caused by internal politics can change people for the worse.

## HAVE I BECOME INSTITUTIONALIZED – AS AN INDIVIDUAL?

1. *Our perceptions change:* Were your initial perceptions of your organization, team and boss positive? More than likely, otherwise you would not have joined them. In order for you to have performed well in your interview or assessment centre, we can assume that so too were your perceptions of yourself. However, it may be that, soon after your honeymoon period, your perceptions began to change. After several months, many of us find ourselves uncharacteristically expending energy, which we would normally use achieving our tasks, on protecting our status by fighting our corner or our 'comfort zone' by unwillingly avoiding, accommodating or competing with others.

2. *Our attitudes change:* When you arrived did you have strong attitudes of how organizations and their people ought to function? As our perceptions of our work environment change, so too do our attitudes towards ourselves, colleagues, leaders, customers, shareholders and so on.

3. *Our self-concept and self-identity change:* If people are disrespectful, inconsiderate or disparaging not only does our attitude towards them change, but we also begin to develop a negative self-concept and self-identity.

4. *We put up defensive barriers to protect our ego:* When our self-concept and self-identity are under siege, we put up barriers to protect our egos. Such ego defensive mechanisms include attacking, blaming or avoiding those whom we perceive as misperceiving us and who have the power to damage our self-concept further.

5. *Our motivation diminishes:* If such needs as achievement, fulfilment, respect, recognition, self-respect and a sense of inclusion are not being satisfied, our motivation will diminish.

6. *Our decision making is less effective:* If there is an unsupportive, critical or ambiguous climate, the quality of our decisions will diminish.

7. *We feel powerless:* Argyris (1973) showed how modern organizations actively frustrate our need for autonomy. McClelland and Burnham, (1995), whose work reflects the same conclusions, identified the need for power as one of the most significant motivational factors in organizations. When we give in to those disproportionately seeking personal power we, in contrast, begin to feel powerless.

8. *We feel isolated:* When we fail to contribute and to participate fully in our environment we become detached from the rest of the group and eventually experience feelings of isolation.

9. *Work – and life – becomes meaningless:* Literally hundreds of research studies by Maier and his associates (1970) demonstrate that participating in group problem solving makes work meaningful and increases satisfaction with the work situation. Clearly the opposite is true. When we opt out of participating in team discussions and thereby allow others to solve our problems and take our decisions, our work becomes meaningless. Satisfying everyone else's needs and neglecting our own results in our lives becoming meaningless.

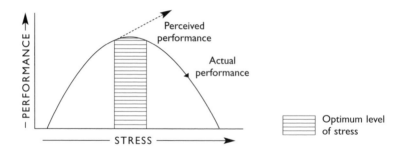

**Figure 3.1**  Relationship between performance and stress

10. *Our stress levels increase:* All these feelings will be displayed in behaviour that may well be bad for ourselves and bad for the organization. Stress can be the result, and the symptoms include decreased performance, absenteeism, alcoholism, migraines, ulcers and depression.

A useful model that illustrates the relationship between stress, on the one hand and performance on the other, is shown in Figure 3.1. It shows how there are two aspects to stress – positive and negative. A difficult task in organizations is to find the optimum point for each individual, which will differ depending on their capacity for stress. As a quick temperature check on morale and job satisfaction, it is worth showing people the model and asking them where they are on this curve. Very few will say they're at the challenged, energized, inspired, can't wait to get out of bed to go to work, optimum level of stress. They are either overloaded or underchallenged, both of which result in decreased performance. Maybe CEOs could try asking this question during a company meeting as a temperature check on the company's effective use of its human potential. And any one of us can use it during appraisals before setting new aims and objectives.

## HAVE I BECOME INSTITUTIONALIZED – AS A TEAM MEMBER?

1. *Group dynamics:* When you joined your team, did you take a while to check out the various roles played by your colleagues before feeling your way into the group? Teams develop their own implicit norms, or ground rules, that are used to regulate the behaviour of their members. As teams develop, the status quo may become very uncomfortable and can have an enormous influence on shaping self-perceptions and hence our team roles and level of participation.

2. *Group membership:* When the team is well balanced, individuals are likely to find the teamwork an enriching experience. Individuals can be adversely affected, however, by deficiencies in the team such as lacking a 'Team Worker' who likes to creates harmony (Belbin, 1993). Then individuals who occasionally need an arm around the shoulder are likely to feel anxious and neglected. Their anxiety may leave them frozen at the edge of the abyss unable to contribute.

3. *Conflict:* Conflict can result in winners and losers with the winners often becoming more self-righteous, overconfident and complacent. The losers, on the other hand, become tense and demoralized and may either look for opportunities to regain their honour or, remaining silent, give in and give up.

4. *Leadership:* Whether the leader of a group has formal authority or is merely able to exert influence without it, their behavioural style has implications for the tone of meetings, the manner tasks are accomplished and the outcomes of the team's endeavours. If you have ever been in a team led at first by a great leader and then by a poor one, you will know how people's behaviour can change almost overnight.

5. *Political tactics:* As I said earlier, political tactics tend to be used to acquire, maintain or enhance power. Political activity is commonplace in many organizations. When people manipulate the team dynamics for their own purpose, at its most destructive it will cause others to either wilt in the face of it or strike back in return.

6. *Corridor meetings:* Do you find it easier to avoid disagreeing in team meetings yet, needing to have your say, tend to voice them in corridor meetings with colleagues you trust? We quickly learn to fit into the culture of the group which includes an implicit rule that arguing loudly in meetings is acceptable by some but not by others.

## HAVE I BECOME INSTITUTIONALIZED – AS A COMPANY MAN OR WOMAN?

1. *Structure:* An organization structure and job design that provide high levels of autonomy, feedback and variety will increase productive efficiency, quality and flexibility (Hackman and Lawler, 1971). But the organization structure can establish regular patterns of behaviour that can militate against two-way communications and quick decisions and leave many frustrated by the formal hierarchy yet equally resentful of

those who bypass it. Frustration can turn to demoralization and an unwillingness to cooperate.

2. *Threats to power:* Regular threats to reduce the power of a group or an individual may result in their uncharacteristically withholding knowledge, arguing, blocking or not delivering.

3. *Communication:* Incomplete or incorrect communication creates uncertainty, rumour, anxiety and defensiveness.

## BREAKING THE THREADS

It is clear that being part of an organization can change people, probably for the worse. We need people to break free from the modern equivalent of the threads that 'held' Gulliver down. We all remember somewhere in the back of our minds, the person we were, the person we could be, the aspirations we had for ourselves and our business. People in organizations know they have more to offer.

People are disenchanted because they work hard, they are dedicated and they do the right thing by the company. They silently strive to live by the values, yet not only do they get overlooked, worse still they get trodden on by those who manipulate the system. This is because the Hijackers are also dedicated – not to their work but to building their reputation and visibility. And because the habitual Shadows are dedicated – not to building their reputation and visibility but to destroying yours!

What we who behave as Lambs or Shadows need to appreciate is that dedication is not enough – if we are to be rewarded for our talents we must have the courage not only to work hard but also to ensure that our voice is heard and our talents are heard of (see Figure 3.2).

**Figure 3.2** Gaining recognition

When we join an organization, from day one we need to swiftly become conscious of how easily we lose ourselves; become acquainted with the people; sum up their motivations; know how to handle them skilfully; be prepared to stand up for ourselves, for what we believe is right and access the courage to do so. Unlike those who succumb to the Gulliver Effect, we will achieve a win–win outcome if we quickly and skilfully:

- Recognize – the signs
- Raise – the issue
- Attack – with skill
- Remedy – collaboratively
- Retain – the organization's values

## HOW DO I BECOME A WARRIOR?

We become a Warrior by mastering the Six Cs. Without these skills, we will be living in a world not of our making, over which we have no control and which has the capacity to frustrate us at every turn.

With the Six Cs we will shape our own world based on our own values and convictions. This will not only be good for us, it will also benefit like-minded colleagues and beyond that, the organization as a whole (Table 3.1). And who knows, it may also benefit our home and social life too.

| | Conflict | Concepts | Collaboration | Consensus | Compassion | Courage |
|---|---|---|---|---|---|---|
| **FOR DEVELOPMENT** | An insight into how conflict impinges on our Inner and Outer Warrior and hence our mode of operating when friction is around | A conceptual framework to diagnose group process – the behaviour and dynamics of any group that works closely together | How to create a collaborative climate where blockages – whether inter-functional, interpersonal or related to business issues – can be tackled and resolved as and when they arise | Skills to remain calm and in control in even the most stressful situations such that you can see both sides of an argument and are prepared to hear and facilitate a win–win agreement | Replace habitual and ineffective responses with ones which facilitate empathic problem solving and commitment to agreed decisions – at both the task and interpersonal levels | A philosophy which will help you find your voice and use the previous 5 Cs, whatever the circumstances, in a determined effort to change your life and work experiences |

**Table 3.1** The Six Cs of the Inner Warrior

## OVERVIEW AND CONCLUSIONS

It should be clear now that people's attitudes, beliefs and behaviours can change soon after they join a company. At worst, the outcome will be many decisions being formulated on non-communitarian grounds. But this will also lead, in many cases, to individuals either opting out of the corporate mainstream or compromising their values in order to protect themselves from potential attacks.

At all times in an organization's life – not simply during or as a result of change – while collaboration, openness and trust exist, so do competitiveness, defensiveness and distrust. It is highly unrealistic to expect that any organization is ever going to function at either extreme.

Thus even in the most humanistic organization there is going to be some internal competition for position, admiration or resources; some wariness on the part of individuals when faced with new or uncertain situations; and some honest dislike of other people. Not recognizing these negative conditions is to miss a trick in increasing loyalty, participation and productivity.

How do we change ourselves back – back to being the brave Warriors we once were before we learnt to adapt to our work environment?

We do this by becoming aware of how we have changed and the impact of our changes on others, the organization and ourselves. We then develop the skills to tap back into our Inner Warrior and behave as the Warrior our organization needs us to be. Not to mention ourselves.

An organization development intervention designed to work at the micro level of the individual is prescribed. However, the change agents used to implement this solution will need to have an explicitly affective focus if this intervention is to succeed. The following two chapters will examine these two aspects of change management.

# CHAPTER 4

# CURRENT CHANGE REMEDIES

## ONGOING RESISTANCE FROM SOME WEARS DOWN DEDICATION OF OTHERS

Many people in our organizations feel undervalued, overwhelmed and struggle constantly. Not because of the difficulties of adapting to large-scale change programmes but because they encounter obstacles everywhere in the organization in simply attempting to effect routine, but necessary, everyday change.

Examples of such changes would be:

- Agreeing a piece of work which involves team members accommodating it into their schedule
- Appealing to colleagues to start meetings on time
- Changing the parking arrangements
- Persuading the *entire* leadership team to hold weekly surgeries to cascade management board decisions
- Trying to squeeze an extra £10,000 out of the finance director for a marketing project during a budget review
- Introducing a 'no smoking' policy
- Seeking to implement improvements to channels of communication during the life of a project team

In all cases progress may be stymied in order to feed the ego of an overly political character. It is *this* dynamic which is endemic to the organization and which, prior to inception, prevents change programmes such as total quality management (TQM) or business process re-engineering (BPR) from succeeding.

There are three main types of ongoing resistance to even the smallest suggestion of change to working practices:

1. *Resistance to the change itself:* rejected because people think it's not worth their time, effort or attention.
2. *Resistance to the change strategy:* (a) using force, for example, may create resistance among individuals who resent management by 'command' (b) some people may resist rational explanations in which they believe the data are suspect (c) others may resist intuitive hunches with insufficient supporting data (d) others may resist a collaborative approach that to them appears manipulative or insincere.
3. *Resistance to the change agent:* This can involve jealousy and other interpersonal differences. People who are aloof from those in the change situation or who appear self-serving and/or who have a high emotional involvement in the changes are especially prone to such problems. Research also indicates that people who differ from others on such dimensions as age, education and socio-economic factors may encounter greater resistance to change (Rogers, 1993).

The norm in many organizations is not to raise the true reasons for resistances in meetings, where they could be resolved. Coch and French (1948) found that people instead complain about frequent changes in their work methods (and, I would suggest, about their encounter with political characters who resist change) via:

- Absenteeism
- Leaving the company
- Low standards of efficiency
- Complaints about pay rates
- Deliberate restriction of output
- Aggression towards management

Other useful measures include:

- High rates of sickness
- Strained interpersonal relationships
- More employee grievances
- Accidents and mistakes
- Changes in physical appearance
- More customer complaints

## 'FELT' VERSUS 'REAL' NEEDS

The effects of our maintaining cultures that squander human potential on internal resistance and competition are made apparent to management through:

| Table 4.1 Felt versus real needs | |
| --- | --- |
| **FELT NEEDS** | **REAL NEEDS** |
| ■ Poor profits<br>■ Loss of customers and increased customer complaints<br>■ Low productivity<br>■ Insufficient sales<br>■ Poor product quality<br>■ Extensive machine downtime<br>■ High inventories<br>■ Late deliveries<br>■ Rising costs<br>■ Non-competitive prices | ■ Bids for power and authority<br>■ Insufficient leadership and managerial skills<br>■ Low morale and cohesion<br>■ Divergent goals and objectives<br>■ Silo-mentality<br>■ Inter-group friction<br>■ Poor communication<br>■ Uncooperative colleagues<br>■ High stress levels<br>■ Feelings of powerlessness and neglect |

- Poor profits
- Insufficient sales
- Extensive machine downtime
- Employee satisfaction surveys
- Customer satisfaction surveys
- 360-degree feedback on managers and leaders

Recognizing and acting on these issues is all well and good. However, too many organizations diagnose wrongly the problems they are keen to address. Frequently solutions are based upon 'felt needs', which relate to technical and operational issues rather than the 'real needs' beneath the surface, which are the people issues (see Table 4.1).

Whilst dealing with the felt needs, the real, underlying problems involving human relations issues of poor communication, bids for power and control and intergroup frictions are likely to come to the surface. When they do emerge, such problems are resolved in the context of operational issues. In other words why many texts on change programmes see the human relations issues as the *result* of resistance to change rather than the surfacing of real problems that *existed* in the organization in the first place.

## CURRENT REMEDIES

A number of key change programmes designed to deal with the felt needs – technical and operational issues – have been established. And sure enough related research has usually concluded that people issues account for their failure.

## Total Quality Management (TQM)

TQM is an organization-wide strategy that focuses on achieving or exceeding customer expectations (Luthans, 1993). Accordingly, quality has become a critical factor (Easton, 1993). But, so too is price, and organizations are keen to achieve a balance between the two. The solution is TQM, which builds quality in during the production process, reducing errors and appraising mistakes which could result in fewer defective products and at a reduced cost.

Most texts argue that realizing TQM's promised advantages is crucially dependent on using human resources in an appropriate way (Macduffie, 1995). So the challenge for firms is to develop both methods that elicit cooperation and commitment and managers who have a supportive, open style; if they cannot accept this way of working, severe problems are likely to be encountered in its installation.

Moreover, there is very strong evidence that the firms who get the best results have recognized that human resource practices such as *empowering the workforce* and *eliciting its cooperation and commitment* are intrinsic to TQM.

## Business Process Re-engineering (BPR)

BPR involves a fundamental rethink and, if necessary, a radical redesigning of business process with the aim of making dramatic improvements to critical aspects of performance such as cost, quality, integration, service and speed. (Hammer and Champy, 1993).

During the early 1990s BPR was embraced by many organizations. But instead of enhancing performance the result amounted to a reduction in profits, in effectiveness and in efficiency (Grey and Mitev, 1995). In each case there was a simple explanation: it has been argued that the commitment, loyalty and teamwork that existed previously were virtually destroyed overnight. So strong was this trend that Davenport, one of the early advocates of BPR, stated that re-engineering had gone seriously wrong and become a 'fad that forgets people' (Davenport, 1992).

### CURRENT RECIPES FOR IMPLEMENTING CHANGE

So when programmes aimed at operational and technical change meet with resistance, the focus switches to the process of change and its successful implementation.

One popular approach to change implementation draws on the methods of *project management*. The typical project life cycle involves the following steps: identify problem, gather data, analyse data, generate solutions, select the best solution, plan the implementation, implement and test, monitor and evaluate. This makes the change process sound like a neat, logical sequence of discrete and identifiable steps. David Collins (1998) refers to these prescriptions as '*N*-step recipes', as different contributors compete to offer checklists of different lengths (with broadly similar content).

According to advocates of this approach, it is useful in specifying the main factors contributing to effective change and offering a checklist of required actions. However, there is a presumption that if change is messy it is because managers have failed to follow the steps. This may not be the case if we consider that most change is intrinsically messy, politicized, untidy, irrational and iterative.

Anyone who has gone through an unsuccessful change programme may well recognize that all these steps were studiously adhered to and still resistance was rife!

Another approach to successful implementation can be found in the *process/contextual theory*. Patrick Dawson (1994) argues that to understand the process of change we need to consider:

1. the past, present and future *context* in which the organization functions (external and internal factors)
2. the *substance* of the change itself – for example new technology, new structure – and its significance and timescale
3. the transition *process*, tasks, activities, decisions, timing, sequencing
4. *political activity*, both within and external to the organization
5. the *interactions* between these factors.

Process/contextual theory recognizes the complexity of change but sees the people involved in the change process as pawns moved around by organizational forces rather than as proactive 'movers and shakers'. In addition, it does not identify practical recommendations for change, beyond generalized advice.

Regardless of the theoretical soundness of a change programme or the way it is implemented, because of the personal experiences at grass-root level, it is doomed to fail. This is not because people resist change – they are simply resistant as a necessary byproduct of the climate in which they find themselves. Conventional perspectives on change do not address the needs of good people working with egocentric colleagues and so they continue to suffer the Gulliver Effect at the hands of those who try to intimidate them.

## PEOPLE-CENTRED CHANGE PROGRAMMES

Nevertheless, when the implementation of BPR and TQM stalls it does provide the impetus for focusing on the human side of organizations. Individuals may attend leadership development, coaching and mentoring, skills training or team-building 'awaydays'. Alternatively, the entire company will go through an integrated change programme such as Empowerment or Organization Development.

# Empowerment

Empowerment acknowledges that those doing the jobs at the sharp end are the most knowledgeable and so are best placed to make decisions affecting customers. Empowerment aims to:

- achieve a higher level of performance by giving people the authority to use their initiative to make and implement their own decisions
- reduce supervision and control by encouraging the use of coaching and mentoring
- embody humanistic values by giving employees autonomy and opportunities for self-development

However, saying that employees are empowered is one thing, empowering them in practice is another. Does it deliver? No! Empowerment often fails to work because managers and supervisors find it hard to let go of the previous way of doing things (Cunningham et al., 1996) and people in these organizations often report feelings of demoralization, demotivation and frustration both before and after change (Holbech, 1994).

# Organization Development (OD)

All of the above programmes left in their wake morale, productivity and resentment that was worse than it had been before. Could it be that, if the real needs were dealt with in the first place, enormous amounts of time money and effort could have been saved? OD is a programme of change that attempts to do just that. It can be defined as:

> A planned, systematic process in which applied behavioural science principles and practices are introduced into organizations, toward the goal of increasing individual and organizational effectiveness. (French and Bell, 1999)

This definition makes it clear that OD promises to deliver two things:

- a happier, more satisfied and more committed workforce
- a more effective organization

OD, then, has a strong focus on matters such as respect for people, trust, collaboration, and participative management. It is concerned with the process of change itself; not only in the process of establishing change but also in staying on top of the adverse natural forces inherent in any environment. In other words, those forces that exist both before, during and after the programme.

OD is a medium- to long-term change strategy that sees the organization as interdependent subsystems. At organizational level this mean using attitude surveys to diagnose the current climate, help shape the mission, vision, values and objectives and measure any before-and-after changes. Often structural redesign is involved.

Because conflict between groups is fairly common in organizations, intergroup interventions usually try to change attitudes to improve interaction between functions and business units. Since OD places a high value on collaborative behaviour, intragroup interventions emphasize team building (Woodman and Sherwood, 1980).

The use of a process consultant to develop more effective groups by helping them to explore potential shortcomings in their own internal processes is central to the OD process. Process consultants model the espoused values of the organization, such as openness, giving and receiving feedback, and showing respect. The hope is that clients will experience the positive impact on their own behaviour and may choose to change by imitation (Golden, 1972).

Because OD focuses on how people work together, it has relatively few techniques targeted on individuals though it may incorporate leadership development, coaching and mentoring.

Does it deliver? Unfortunately, the majority of research conducted to assess the success of OD tends to be of questionable methodological soundness (Beer and Walton, 1987) and, as Terpstra (1981) notes, the more rigorous the research study, the less likely it is that it will find evidence that supports OD's assertions about increased performance and satisfaction.

## THE ACTUAL ENVIRONMENT BEFORE (AND AFTER) THE CHANGE PROGRAMME

Change programmes do not then, appear to improve the morale, collaboration, participation, satisfaction or autonomy of employees, or at least, not for long. Typical group feelings and behaviour remain forever characterized by the following:

- Opting out
- Creative ideas
- Point scoring
- Hidden agendas
- Not listening
- Aggression
- Pockets of collaboration
- Lying
- Fear
- Playing to the crowd
- Humour
- Non-cooperation
- Tension
- Frustration
- Jealousy
- Compromise

- Pairing
- Obstruction
- Mocking
- Confusion
- Constructive disagreements
- Passion
- Patronizing
- Deferring
- Rejecting
- Shallow agreements
- Broken commitments
- Blaming
- Cynicism
- Passivity
- Avoidance
- Manipulation

When the atmosphere is bad, we feel powerless in the face of what we see before us, yet the sense of powerless is in our heads since we could stand up and be counted if we only knew how.

## OVERVIEW AND CONCLUSION

Since the early 1950s and the rise of the human relations movement, much emphasis has been placed on the need for and importance of participation and collaboration in the organizational setting. This is the culture espoused not only by OD consultants but also that of BPR, TQM, Empowerment and so on.

I believe that emphasis has been useful – but incomplete.

Those of you who read my first book *Confronting Company Politics* (1997) may recall that I argue that, rather than focus on making the organization safer, pleasanter or easier for the individual a more productive approach would be to help individuals recognize, develop and experience their own potency and ability to cope, whatever the present condition. In this way they will not be browbeaten by the person in the corridor who confronts them or the Hijacker in the meeting whose agenda overrides everyone else's.

# CHAPTER 5

# ON BECOMING A WARRIOR

## DON'T REARRANGE THE CHAIRS

Imagine we have one team and two process consultants. After half an hour of observing the team working, one process consultant notices that certain members of the team are looking bored, frustrated or fidgety. She asks everyone what they think the problems are.

Immediately the atmosphere is one of alertness; noticeably this also applies to those previously disengaged. Reasons given are that the agenda is not adhered to. They have overrun the timed session and have no idea what the objectives are for the current discussion.

This process consultant sees these complaints – the felt needs – as the real needs and helps solve them at a task level by moving the team on to the next item on the agenda. In effect, they are rearranging the chairs.

The second process consultant says to herself, 'These complaints are the symptoms of underlying authority issues and the Gulliver Effect' – the real needs. She sees the disaffected people as divided into two sets:

1. The first set are the Lambs and Shadows. They are acting as *dependent child-like individuals*. Though showing non-verbally that they don't understand where the leader is going with the conversation, they assume he knows best, so say nothing – and instead opt out and stare into space.
2. The second set are the Hijackers. They are acting as *counterdependent adolescent-like individuals* who assume all leaders are incompetent but are damned if they'll help out – so joined in the discussion but unhelpfully, with 'attitude'.

This process consultant bears in mind at all times that she is there to develop individuals who display the values of the organization; these are embodied in the third set of people:

3. These are Warriors, the *interdependent adults*. They have the courage and skills to stop the conversation and ask in an amenable manner how people are feeling about the direction the meeting is taking.

If the job of process consultants is to help individuals collectively create the culture that reflects the organizational values, then they have not only to understand the significance of group dynamics, but also to be able to model the warrior-like behaviours and develop these behaviours in others. A Warrior can see what a non-warrior cannot. Their objective must be to help others acquire warrior-like powers of perception. In this way they will be able to pick up information, interpret it and act accordingly. When everyone can do this, they will then:

■ Recognize – the signs
■ Raise – the issue
■ Attack – with skill
■ Remedy – collaboratively
■ Retain – the organization's values

If we are to have a company of warriors we need interventions at this level of skill.

We can describe the first type as a *cognitive process consultant* (CPC) working with *content issues* and processing the discussion at the task level; and the second type as an *affective process consultant* (APC) working with the underlying human relations *process issues*.

## THERE ARE PROCESS CONSULTANTS AND PROCESS CONSULTANTS

When an objective in an organization is failing, be it cutting costs, completing a project on time or hitting financial targets, the CPC will work with content issues. She will do this by first asking what the task consists of, why it is necessary, when it must be achieved and so on. Once consensus around this strategy is achieved, the next step is to ensure that all the systems and procedures are coordinated and appropriate for goal achievement.

1. *Task*
■ What
■ Why

- When, and so on

2. *Systems and procedures*
- Rules
- Regulations
- Strategy
- Structure and so on
- Process model

However, you can have the best systems and procedures in the world but, as we saw in Chapter 3, if people feel disaffected they won't make them work.

Think back to the times when you have been asked to use a new method of working, one which you had little or no say in establishing. How did it make you feel? Probably you felt resentful, undervalued, unrecognized and not heard. As a consequence how did you behave? Probably you were disinclined to use the system as it was intended. Even if it was an outstanding system. These are the human relations issues.

3. *Human relations*
- 'No one listens to us'
- 'We feel undervalued'
- 'I feel my efforts go unrecognized'
- 'No one communicates'
- 'What's the point?'

In this case the journey from A to B shown in Figure 5.1 will be a turbulent one. An APC would recognize that these human relations issues require as much urgent attention as the task issues and those surrounding the systems and procedures.

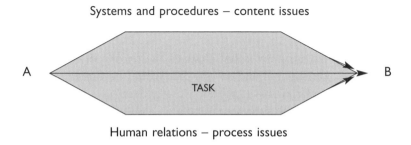

Systems and procedures – content issues

A                                                                    B

TASK

Human relations – process issues

**Figure 5.1** The Hamburger model

*Source:* Developed from Cockman et al., 1999

APCs raise the real issues in the real meeting and bridge the gap between coffee machine culture and meeting culture. Working at this level of intuition and knowledge, they raise the underlying dysfunctional group dynamics that block people being everything they could be.

## THE ILLUSION OF PROGRESS

Unfortunately, these human relations issues frequently do not get raised by process consultants. This leaves people with merely the illusion of progress.

It must be said that many CPCs do uncover issues that escape normal communication channels. The following are typical of the kind of information that is gathered in meetings facilitated by them:

- The lines of reporting are unclear. To whom is allegiance due? What are my priorities?
- Some managers are very inaccessible and inapproachable
- I find it difficult to work around our silo-mentality
- No one communicates face-to-face any more. Should we ban the use of emails?
- Setting realistic budgets is a tortuous process. How can I simplify things?

Corrective actions on many of the issues identified are not difficult to set in motion. Not only that but also these interventions do contribute to helping a participative culture.

Sometimes these interventions involve a hundred or more representatives from the organizations and require a two-day conference. The CPC will begin by setting out the importance of honesty, openness and respect for others during the process. The steps proceed as flows:

1. Participants are divided into cross-functional subgroups of five or six individuals.
2. Each group has an hour to list changes in any aspect of the business (objectives, procedures and so on) that would be organizationally or personally beneficial.
3. Using flipcharts, each subgroup reports its list to the total group.
4. Then, in plenary, the consultant facilitates the classification of the proposed changes into categories.
5. New subgroups, each led by a key manager and his followers, meet for three purposes.

- To select the three and determine what action they will take
- To select the items top management should assign highest priority
- To plan for communicating to absent colleagues

6. Each subgroup reports its conclusions in plenary. The CEO and leadership team make decisions, though possibly only tentatively. Follow-up planning ends the meeting.

Beckhard (1969) calls this approach a *confrontation meeting*. But in fact it simply involves a one-day activity, designed to suspend formal lines of communication and decision making and make it possible to bring together diverse segments of the organization for diagnosis, priority setting, and action recommendations.

It does not, however, involve confrontation. Rather, 'anonymous, more or less off-the-cuff feedback is forwarded to a higher-level group from lower level personnel' (Blake and Mouton, 1983).

## THE RISK OF SUPERFICIALITY

The problem with this kind of development activity is that it runs the risk of superficiality because:

1. Time is insufficient for deep analysis of content issues.
2. If participants encounter process issues in the subgroups or plenary, the concept of dealing with those issues is not on the radar of the CPC.
3. The temptation to compromise is high and so ownership of the output and responsibility for following through are low.

Accordingly, people become excited in the group sessions but later on feel let down because the changes they expected have not occurred.

This approach generates an initial unloading that is at least quasi-cathartic, interspersed with encouragement calculated to make participants aware of their own attempts to escape from painful frankness. Promoting harmony through congeniality and turning away from the real problem by concentrating on areas where few or no problems exist may be enjoyable but is not likely to be productive (Blake and Mouton, 1983).

## TRANSIENT CHANGE

The fact that these issues do not get raised means that any changes are transient. For long-term change we need to recognize, raise, attack, remedy and remain vigilant to signs of the Gulliver Effect. So let's re-examine Gulliver's group experience with the Lilliputians.

> I confess I was often tempted, while they (the Lilliputians) were passing backwards and forwards on my Body, to seize forty or fifty of the first that came in my reach, and dash them against the ground. But the remembrance of *what I'd felt*, which probably might not be the worst they could do, and the *promise of honour I made them*, for so I interpreted my submissive behaviour, soon drove out these imaginations. (Swift, 2003, my emphasis)

From this excerpt, it is striking how Gulliver rationalizes doing nothing. He uses a misplaced sense of honour (to the Lilliputians) and a fear of pain recurring to opt out of acting decisively.

An APC running a 100-strong group meeting would be alert to every non-verbal nuance and paralinguistic sign – tone of voice, speed of delivery and so on. If they noticed a team member suppressing rejection of another's contribution (possibly out of a misplaced sense of honour to their status in the organization or for fear of retribution) they would seek to address it immediately. Even the most trivial, ill-at-ease interaction may have enormous significance and reverberate far beyond the confines of the meeting room.

In other words, in order to run a successful meeting we should be focusing on the Gulliver Effect.

In addition, we need to know how to retain what we've learnt and apply the principles in our everyday work and life. It is unrealistic to expect to be able to go back as a changed person and expect it to work just like that. The people we work with have an investment in our staying the same.

Coming back to Gulliver then, it suited the Lilliputians for him to remain a submissive Lamb or a Shadow. By waiting until his emotions ran high he made the change unskilfully as a Hijacker. The alternative would have been for him to communicate as a Warrior. How, then could he have made this change?

He could have said: 'I'm going to stand up now. I'm prepared to negotiate how I do that so that it causes you all as little disruption as possible.

To which the Lilliputians would have said: 'We don't want you to stand up, it suits us for you to stay lying down.'

Gulliver should then have replied, 'I can't lie here until I die – I've got to be me.'

For Gulliver to achieve a win–win with the Lilliputians he needed to have the *courage* to negotiate a *collaborative*, *consensus* agreement to stand up and be himself.

People who attend training and development may well have made a plan inside their head to make a change. This is why they leave with energy and good intentions. Then they return to the group after having agreed in their own minds to make a change, but do not communicate this to the other members of the group. When they do eventually act, they do not get the right response; and so real group change and, by implication, organizational change remain out of reach. Without courage, if the group is unsupportive and reacts negatively, it doesn't take much for the individual to revert to their former self. This is where many training and development programmes fall down. This is why nothing changes.

We cannot allow our people to sit around Gulliver-like in groups. We need APCs who can help individuals make changes to their behaviour that can be sustained in the long term back at the ranch.

## SOCIAL FACTS: AN INNOVATIVE FORM OF DATA

One reason that process issues are neglected is that often people are not skilled in the gathering and analysis of relevant information. Through observation, interview or intuition, the APC can fill this gap. Data need not be physical facts: often data consist of 'social facts' – attitudes and emotions – gathered through interviews, observation and intuition. The presumption here is that feelings are information. Once recognized, we can incorporate them in the search for solutions. Thus feelings and emotions can be surfaced and presented informationally, without fear of a negative response. This kind of communication about 'feelings as data' gives each person additional information essential for interpersonal problem solving.

Yet those who opt to work in groups have an obligation to care for other members, help create a supportive environment and help others understand how they are perceived and whether they are helpful or harmful in the way they communicate.

> **Feelings about relationships as facts**
>
> ▪ Need to recognize they are data – their significance
> ▪ Need to know how to gather them – using intuition

We need APCs who can point out when people are evading important issues or avoiding expressions of feelings. They can also give support and protection to those who find it difficult to function in a group. This latter function is particularly relevant where there are real or perceived differences in the use of power and authority within the group. Feelings and emotions may be too deep to be channelled constructively. Under these conditions an interventionist approach that moderates tensions and provides a way forward is advocated.

## OVERVIEW AND CONCLUSION

In order to eradicate the Gulliver Effect, we need affective process consultants (APCs) who can create a safe climate and point out group processes. They can then help people to awaken their Inner Warrior. Once this is awake in us, we will have the courage to skilfully fight for what is right in accordance with our values and those of the organization. I do not advocate the use of 'touchy feely' process consultants who, in the words of Woody Allen, are very 'involved with themselves'! We are seeking APCs who courageously confront the saboteurs and develop those who acquiesce because when it comes to group process, they look but cannot not see.

We should all by now understand how important it is for us and our organization to be authentic. And that this equally requires the courage of our convictions in the absence of the facilitator. There are a number of simple behaviours which team members can employ to promote better functioning within the group. Perhaps the most important among them is a willingness to share how things are and seem for them personally and by displaying a corresponding willingness to accept how it is and seems for others. Groups in which members show this willingness tend to function with greater satisfaction for those taking part.

It does happen sometimes, however, that someone who is honest and open about the way things are for them is badly treated and comes away from the experience reluctant to try it out again for fear of being put down, ignored or rejected. One way to eliminate this is to have leaders who are warrior-like in the face of self-serving opponents.

Yet, the Gulliver Effect occurs at every level of an organization including the boardroom. Before we embark upon a step-by-step approach to acquiring the Six Cs, the following chapter will look at how leadership can influence development in our organizations.

# CHAPTER 6

# COMPASSIONATE LEADERSHIP

## LOOKING OUTWARD *AND* INWARD

> Something appears to be missing. Successful leaders seem to be outnumbered by the unsuccessful ones.
>
> *(Morris et al., 1995)*

Try and think of a leader as a role model and, like most texts, you may first think of Martin Luther King and John F. Kennedy in the USA and Winston Churchill and Lord Sieff of Marks & Spencer in the UK; all of whom are no longer with us. Next you may think of Richard Branson – with reservations. He, like the others, appears to hold a vision that balances a drive to achieve the task at hand with a concern for people.

When pushed for more names, those we recall probably enjoy their status for their ability to deliver a compelling vision. They have a certain charisma and are highly skilled communicators. Indeed, most texts define a leader as 'an individual who knows where he or she is going and is able to *persuade others to go willingly* with them' (Barron and Greenberg, 1990; Kotter, 1998; Rollinson, 2002).

When you look inside their organizations, however, what appears to be lacking is a forceful follow-through on the delivery of the visions they present. It's all very well their gazing, in effect, at a distant utopia and inspiring others to follow, but if they do not look behind them some six weeks later to ask 'What are you all doing running around in circles playing games?' their vision will not be successfully implemented. Organizations, teams, people – all need to be led by individuals who are able to look *inwardly* as well outwardly.

My definition adds that leaders equally need to persuade people to do so *as a team of like-minded individuals*. In other words, the function of leaders is not only to capture the support of individuals in achieving the tasks of the business by leveraging energy, confidence and goodwill. Having allotted the tasks, leaders must also vigilantly compel the troops to work collaboratively together to action them. To achieve their vision, our leaders must protect the weak, redirect the egocentric, and reward those who struggle to remain strong.

This applies as much to their peers in the boardroom as to the people elsewhere in the organization. We need leaders who are prepared to play a central role in the eradication of the Gulliver Effect both:

(a) amongst their followers, *and*
(b) within their own leadership team

Those we name as great leaders have the compassion to indulge people with diametrically opposed styles and the foresight to encourage and value their contributions. They *recognize* the real needs – human relations issues – that block progress on tasks, *raise* them courageously, *attack* them skilfully, and *remedy* them collaboratively whilst *remaining vigilant* in ensuring that their values are lived not laminated; having zero tolerance of anything less.

## HEARTS AND MINDS

Is leadership important? The answer to this question is most evident when the same group of people underachieve under one leader and excel under another. Many of us have known teachers whose manner inspired us to be confident, take risks and learn. We have also known teachers who created, within that same class, a fearful atmosphere in which our main concern was for covering our backs. So what makes an effective leader?

There are umpteen theories of leadership each of which focuses on different variables. In the 1920s, *trait theories* attempted to list those personality traits that leaders possessed, but failed to produce results – merely long lists and unclear definitions. In the 1940s, the *functional approach* looked at what leaders actually *do*, that is, their behaviour or style. But since it became clear that there was more than one effective style, in the 1960s *contingency theory* was born, which argues that the appropriate style is dependent on the situation.

In the 1980s, the leadership role models were action-oriented, charismatic individuals such as Jack Welch and Rupert Murdoch. They were distinguishable from managers by their ability to communicate effectively, lead by example and create an engaging vision. Such *transactional leaders* emphasize clarity of goals and objectives and of rewards and punishments.

Their relationships are based on a negotiated mutual dependence: 'I will give you this, if you do that' (Birkinshaw and Crainer, 2002).

This profusion of theories and models led McGregor (1987) to conclude that 'leadership is not a property of the individual, but a complex relationship among (numerous) variables'. Key variables include characteristics of the manager and followers; structure, function and culture of the organization; and the social, economic and political environment.

There may be no one 'best' form of leadership, but the changing nature of organizations including an emphasis on work–life balance; increased internal competition; demanding customers; and the prevailing importance of business ethics and social responsibility have resulted in a call for an environment of coaching, support and empowerment. The relationship is therefore not simply one of leader behaviour that results in subordinate behaviour but an interdependent one that relies on the willingness of the follower to trust in and abide by what he is being told.

Remember, you can be appointed a manager but you are not a leader until your appointment is 'ratified in the hearts and minds of those who work for you' (Adair, 1986).

## THE IDEAL LEADER

So, in the 1990s the concept of *transformational leadership* began which emphasized the leader's ability to appeal to higher ideals and values of followers, and create a feeling of *justice, loyalty and trust*. Such theorists have come almost full circle back to trait theories whereby excellent leaders are said to possess certain qualities and styles. William Pearce (1991), a Westinghouse executive, advocated *'soft' leadership*, stressing the importance of *openness, sensitivity and vulnerability*. Daniel Goleman (1995), best-selling author of *Emotional Intelligence*, advocated the five components of EQ as: *self-awareness, self-regulation, motivation, empathy and social skill*. At the London Business School, Rob Goffee and Gareth Jones (2002) argue that inspirational leaders have high levels of *authenticity, self-awareness, intuition, empathy and selectively show their weaknesses*.

This 'New Leadership' is succinctly summarized by Birkinshaw and Crainer (2002) in describing the three key aspects of Sven-Goran Eriksson's style as: *situation sensing* – sniffing out signals and sensing what is going without it being spelled out; *authenticity* – staying true to yourself, so nothing you do seems fake; and *empathy* – ability to identify with team members, but also know when and how to pull back and take a more authoritative position.

The New Leadership, then, advocates leaders who can:

- Sense the situation – intuitive, decisive, inspirational
- Know and remain true to themselves – authentic, self-aware, self-revelatory, socially skilled, selectively show weaknesses, open
- Know and empathize with others – empathic, good communicators, motivators, socially skilled, sensitive

Do our business leaders possess these qualities and styles? The short answer is No. The research shows that very few of our leaders have these styles of relating to themselves, others or the world.

In a survey carried out by OPP in 2002, 1000 UK workers ranked leaders' desirable qualities in the following order: trust, communication skills, decisiveness and the ability to motivate and inspire. Yet whilst 69 per cent ranked trust as essential only 20 per cent believed trust to be their boss's strongest quality. The other qualities were similarly ranked low on being enacted. This is worrying when today's leaders are called upon to lead by example and demonstrate good people skills.

## OPPOSING STRENGTHS

One way to understand leadership styles is to use the MBTI (Myers-Briggs Type Indicator). The MBTI (Myers, 1962) is the most commonly used personality test; it looks at differences in personal style in four different areas:

1. Introversion   Extroversion   – how we get and use our energy
2. Sensing        iNtuition      – how we gather and take in information
                                    to understand our world
3. Thinking       Feeling        – how we make our decision once the
                                    information is gathered
4. Judging        Perceiving     – how we organize our lives; speed of and
                                    adherence to decisions

The following describe each area:

- *Introverts* find energy in the inner world of ideas, concepts and abstractions.
- *Extroverts* find energy in things and people, preferring interactions with others and action.
- *Sensing* people prefer to take in information through their five senses and are detail oriented, want facts and trust them. Joe Friday in the TV show *Dragnet* is a good example – all he ever wanted was 'just the facts'.

- *iNtuitives* seek out patterns and relationships, sense information through a 'gut feel', trust hunches and look for the big picture. Albert Einstein, whose experiments revolutionized the 20th century, could see patterns where others saw randomness or chaos.

- *Thinking* people decide things impersonally on analysis, logic and principle. They value justice and fairness. Mr Spock, science officer of the starship *Enterprise* exemplifies the Thinking type.

- *Feeling* people decide by focusing on human values. They value harmony and compassion, are good at persuasion and facilitating differences among group members. Dr McCoy, Spock's colleague, demonstrated a preference for Feeling.

- *Judging* people are decisive, planful and self-regimented. Deadlines are sacred. Their motto is: Just do it!

- *Perceptive* people are curious, adaptable, and spontaneous. They start many tasks, and deadlines are meant to be stretched. Their motto is: On the other hand...

The two poles for each of the four dimensions yield 16 basic personality types, for example ESTJ, ENFJ and so on. Each combination has detailed explanations, but here I will focus on the findings of the research on leadership using MBTI.

It can be seen that iNtuitive Feeling (NF) types possess the qualities of the New Leadership. ENFPs can be described as follows:

NF people are enthusiastic innovators, always seeing new possibilities and new ways of doing things. They have a lot of imagination and initiative for starting projects, and a lot of impulsive energy for carrying them out. They are stimulated by difficulties and are most ingenious at solving them.

Their enthusiasm gets other people interested too. Their feeling judgment can add depth to the insights supplied by their intuition. Their feeling preference shows in a concern for people. They are skilful in handling people and often have remarkable insight into the possibilities and development of others. They are extremely perceptive about the attitudes of others, aiming to understand rather than judge people. (Extracts from *Introduction to Type*. Consulting Psychologists Press Inc., distributed by Oxford Psychologists Press)

## WHAT LEADERS DO WE HAVE?

Do our business leaders possess the NF qualities? Research on leadership using the MBTI demonstrates that, in fact, most of our leaders are Sensing Thinking (ST) types. ESTJs can be described as follows:

STs are people who use their thinking to run as much of the world as may be theirs to run. They enjoy executive action and long-range planning. Reliance on thinking makes them logical, analytical, objectively critical and not likely to be convinced by anything but reasoning. They tend to focus on ideas, not the person behind the ideas.

They think conduct should be ruled by logic, and govern their own behaviour accordingly. They live by a definite set of rules that embody their basic judgments about the world. Any change in their ways requires a deliberate change in their rules. (Extracts from *Introduction to Type*. Consulting Psychologists Press Inc., distributed by Oxford Psychologists Press)

Clearly it is the NFs who possess the New Leadership qualities. However, Harvey Brightman (2002) shows how 67 per cent of the database of business students at Georgia State University are STs. The latest research from OPP (2002) suggests that 28 per cent (the majority) of leaders in the UK are ST. Margerison and Lewis (1981) surveyed 849 managers attending business school short courses and found that 44.5 per cent were STs, whereas only 6 per cent were NFs. Significantly, NFJs (who nearest resemble the New Leadership) were not represented on the list. So STJs form the largest number of the senior and middle managers and NFPs the least.

People want leaders they can trust and they currently do not believe that is what they have. To have integrity, to be genuine, to communicate authentically and to be in harmony with your self are all central values for NFs. There must be no mask, no deception, no playing of roles. This may be why many leave their organizations to excel as leaders in the family business, or as entrepreneurs starting their own businesses (Kiersey and Bates, 1984). As Carl Rogers puts it:

Becoming a Person means an individual ... moves away from being what he is not, from being a façade. He is not trying to be more than he is, with the attendant feelings of security or bombastic defensiveness. He is not trying to be less than he is, with the attendant feelings of guilt or self-depreciation. He is increasingly listening to the deepest recesses of his psychological and emotional being, and finds himself increasingly willing to be, with greater accuracy and depth, that self which he most truly is. (Rogers, 1961)

Although this description is seen by other styles as 'at best speaking in riddles, and at worst sheer nonsense', it is revered by the NF (Kiersey and Bates, 1984). STs, being predominately concerned with the concrete and specific rather than the ambiguous and abstract, are impatient and distrust issues that to them seem nebulous and not based on tangible facts.

## STs AND COMMUNICATION

It is worth noting that communication is one of the main things that people complain is lacking in their organizations. According to a survey by Deloitte-Touche (2003), CEOs see effective internal communications as number one on their agenda and have called upon HR to focus on this. This has always fascinated me since people will simultaneously complain that:

- 'No one communicates with us'
- 'I receive 120 emails a day!'

People do communicate all the time. Leaders hold company meetings and management conferences; there are company newsletters and in-house magazines, and team meetings are held so often that no one ever seems to be by their phone! Then there are the phone calls, memos, the emails and so on.

When individuals complain that no one communicates, in focus groups designed to clarify the issues, I have found that what they are really saying is that no one *listens*. And if you probe deeper, the underlying corollary to this is the feeling that 'No one values me', 'No one recognizes my contributions', 'No one cares'.

Could this perception have anything to do with the leadership of our Sensing Thinking types?

For ST people the goal of communicating is to get to the bottom line, to be efficient and not to waste time. They want to get the job done. When STs communicate in this fashion, others may not understand the motivation, but instead may experience the STs' communication as:

- blunt
- rude
- giving orders
- being non-collaborative – not inviting ideas or participation
- impersonal and cold – ignoring personal relationships

But what of the NFs?

## NFs AND COMMUNICATION

For NF types the goal of communication is to engage your attention, energy, and commitment to their ideas and beliefs. They may use analogies, metaphors, and stories from their personal experience to illustrate their point. This appears to be in line with the new leadership qualities of creating and communicating an inspiring vision.

However, when NFs communicate in this way, other types may not recognize or understand the motivation, but instead may experience the communication as:

- rambling
- unclear
- overly optimistic and idealistic
- irrelevant to the task at hand
- too intense

## WHAT DO FOLLOWERS THINK?

Both types make a valuable contribution, yet both styles can generate complaints from their followers. The major contributions ST leaders make are:

- they get to the point and stay focused
- you know where they stand
- they remain calm and self-assured
- they take action to implement decisions
- they are fair and consistent – have systematic principles and stick to them
- work is organized

Yet the major complaints from followers are that ST leaders:

- leave them out of decision making unless their views are directly relevant
- speak bluntly and it can feel like a personal attack
- may move to action before others are ready
- won't bend the rules for anyone – focus on justice rather than compassion
- focused on task completion

The major contributions of NFs are:

- their personal vision is tied to their values and beliefs
- they include others in decision making – want to know what others want/need
- approachable, want to hear what you have to say – draw out and involve others
- they are loyal – very supportive of others and organizational values

- they strive for consensus, build it well and organize the work environment to be harmonious
- they want all employees to get what they want and need

The impact of this is for some followers to complain that NF leaders:

- avoid tough decisions, especially those that will affect people negatively
- don't give the bad news
- may avoid confronting difficult people
- can become moralistic about their personal values expecting everyone to abide by them
- can focus on relationships to the extent that it interferes with task completion

The approach of each type, being so essentially different, will lead to difficulties in communication between them in the boardroom and amongst their followers. In other words, neither appears to fulfil leadership criteria that will satisfy all colleagues and followers.

## A RECIPE FOR THE GULLIVER EFFECT

However, since NFs who possess the so-called soft skills of the New Leadership are besieged by the majority of STs who do not, it is no wonder that the Gulliver Effect is present from the boardroom down. Within management teams what we find is that around the boardroom table sit the same four types: the Hijacker, the Lamb, the Shadow and the Warrior.

It is easy to see that, in the absence of conscious decisions about working together, such team members are likely to assume that what others want from interpersonal communications and teamworking is the same as what they want. If these issues are not discussed, these assumptions and type preferences of the majority of leaders will take over the culture of the business. As a result, some perspectives will be ignored and certain individuals will be underutilized. This, in turn, may cause bad feelings, no notice to be taken of allotted tasks and a remoteness in team meetings.

## BRIDGING THE GAP

## Use Both Types as Dual Leaders

It is understandable that these days, because of the highly competitive nature of the business environment, leaders' eyes are generally fixed on bottom-line short-term performance. Our leaders concern themselves primarily with the hard, tangible features of the organization such as productivity, quality and costs, rather than intangibles such as attitudes openness and trust (McCourt, 1997). However, if our strengths lie on the operational side of the business, then it might be wise to have a number two whose strengths are in people skills.

A number of authors have discussed the need for different types of conceptual style within the management team. Mintzberg (1976) in his article 'Planning on the Left Side, Managing on the Right' shows how managers with a developed left hemisphere more are much better at planning and analytical work whereas managers with developed right hemispheres are better at emotional and imaginative work. Leavitt (1975) also comes to the conclusion that 'we need to integrate wisdom and feeling with analysis'. In other words, we need both Thinking and Feeling types on our leadership teams.

Currently our boards of directors and management teams consist of the following, where 'T' indicates left-brain, task-oriented leaders and 'P' indicates right-brain, people-oriented individuals:

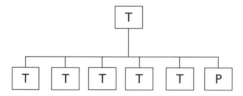

Many people in the organization look up to and are inspired by the people-oriented leader who has captured their hearts and minds. Yet I have found that in times of trouble this is the first person they 'let go'. A well-rounded approach to leadership would mean an executive team resembling the following:

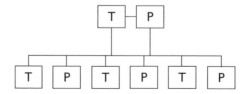

## Appreciate the Wisdom of the Difference

If we are to capitalize on the wisdom of the differences around the table, we need leaders who appreciate that logic, justice and sticking to principles are not enough. Sometimes, we have a moral obligation to indulge those colleagues who see their world of work differently from ourselves. This moral obligation overrides left-brained thinking in the terms of principles, rules and justice.

To create a climate where everybody's views are heard and considered, where intimidation is reduced, our leaders truly need to sense the situation, know themselves, know others and have the courage to eradicate the Gulliver Effect. NFs have the compassion and, possibly as a result, neither the will nor the courage to confront the games. STs have the courage and the will to confront but not the compassion – to appreciate the wisdom of the difference. STs will need to understand the group dynamics and NFs will need to raise them!

The New Leadership qualities of (1) knowing and remaining true to ourselves (2) knowing and empathizing with others and (3) sensing the situation are simply not enough. Many people in our organizations have these qualities, but you'd never know it! We also require a strong connection to our value system and philosophy so that we are urged to act. This is illustrated in Figure 6.1.

Leadership and management development programmes generally work at one or all of the outer layers of this model. Without also raising people's consciousness of the significance of their Inner Warrior in securing the courage to live these values and competencies, we are unlikely to see a significant shift in their leadership behaviour.

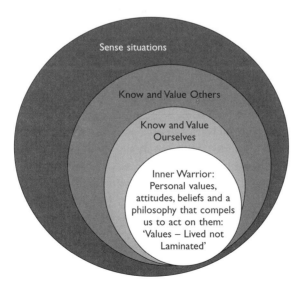

**Figure 6.1** The components of effective leadership

## Soft skills are *hard* to learn! Select leaders who possess them

It is worth considering the reasons for the apparent lack of soft skills amongst our senior management teams. It starts at entry into the system where certain personality characteristics are employed at the cost of others. For example, a successful sales executive scores high on the personality scales of 'competitiveness' and 'achievement'. He does not, as a rule, score high on 'caring' about the feelings of others, but will have sufficient 'creativity' to look as if it is so.

He gets promoted to sales manager on the strength of his sales results. His job now is not only to sell but also to manage and develop his sales team. This now requires the individual to use both task and people skills within the organization. As team leader he now has to understand and care for his team.

If he is successful as a sales manager, he will be promoted to sales director. Now he does no selling – task – at all. His goals have changed. Now his goals must be to persuade the finance director to push customer contracts through as quickly as possible, the marketing director to provide good leads, and the HR director to select excellent staff. He also has to ensure that the staff justify their selection. He may equally want to influence and impress his boss, if he is one day to achieve the ultimate leadership role, that of CEO. He now has to be a team player.

As leaders, we need to recognize that we are now working at a different level and that those skills that got us into the management team are no longer the ones that will keep us there. We need to employ different skills if we are to make a significant contribution to the organization. As a sales person, our contribution was to be a creative, competitive achiever so as to hit our sales targets. Now we have to both influence colleagues and show compassion in listening to and satisfying their problems. This progression is illustrated in Figure 6.2.

I've never understood why we speak of human relations skills as 'soft skills' since we have seen that they are notoriously hard to develop. Surely it is the wrong way around? How much easier it would be for an NF leader to learn the so-called hard skills of balancing an end of year statement or writing a detailed strategic plan.

Selecting more leaders with so-called soft skills who later fill gaps in their knowledge of business administration would be an excellent solution to building a more balanced leadership team. This is especially true given the fact that whereas task-focused people tend to imagine they are strong on the people skills side of leadership (even when their employees know otherwise), people-oriented leaders typically know they are weak on the operational side and are not afraid to seek help to compensate.

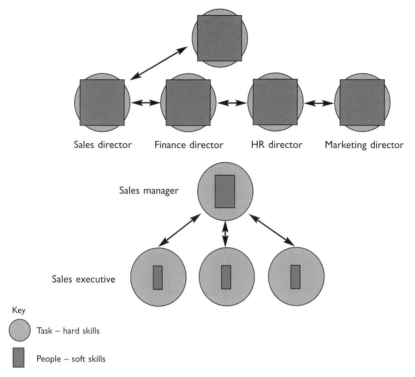

Sales director    Finance director    HR director    Marketing director

Sales manager

Sales executive

Key

Task – hard skills

People – soft skills

**Figure 6.2** The leadership progression

## OVERVIEW AND CONCLUSION

I have frequently observed leaders compete to hijack meetings with their peers. This results in the would-be Warriors indulging them whilst no reciprocal compassion is shown by Hijackers towards them. Passionate, right-brained, visionary types who deal in the wider picture are overpowered by the left-brain logic of those who prefer rational, detailed plans. When they are finally offered an olive branch their optimism and vitality has been drained. Meanwhile, others – Lambs and Shadows – suffering from the Gulliver Effect sit watching in silence.

Armed with the knowledge of the significance of a lack of courage amongst some, leaders will learn to deploy new behaviour patterns. They will develop sensitivity as to how their behaviour can encourage or discourage effective group working. This will result in group behaviours that are in line with the 'laminated' values of respect, open communication and honesty. Everyone will then be adept at using the wisdom of the differences in the group, rather than being insensitive to them.

Leadership development programmes that attempt to establish a single unifying culture by having everyone acquire the same values are unrealistic to some degree. It is unreasonable to expect an authoritarian, risk-averse finance director to lead a successful sales team and equally you would not wish your risk-taking, entrepreneurial, detail-averse sales director to be in charge of finance. There are certain fundamental differences.

Yet, the overriding common value that we must all accept is the right to articulate our beliefs – to value diversity such that we all have the right to access our Inner Warrior and speak without fear. Once the advantages of creating room for everyone on the management team to be heard are felt, leaders will want to encourage similar changes within their own functions and lines of business.

If we are to utilize all of the talent in the organization our leaders need to mobilize the troops, and ensure that they are working in their teams effectively – top down. We therefore need leaders who have the skills of the APC to *recognize* the wisdom of the differences, *raise* those group dynamics which work to suppress them, *attack* them in such a way that they can be *remedied*. Our leaders also need to *remain vigilant*, with zero tolerance of anything less.

If we are to create a climate that encourages the warrior-like behaviours of compassion, indulgence and experimentation we need to develop leaders who:

(a)  can distinguish between Lambs, Shadows, Hijackers and Warriors
(b)  can recognize the behaviours
(c)  can create a senior executive team climate that rewards courage in conflict
(d)  demonstrate the benefits to leaders of doing the same in their functional teams
(e)  have zero tolerance for those who pursue personal agendas.

Only in this way, will values be lived – not laminated.

But we cannot wait for our leaders to do all the work. We all need to take the lead and:

■  Sense the situation
■  Know ourselves
■  Know others
■  Have the courage to eradicate the Gulliver Effect

The seven chapters that make up Part II, The Solution, will explain how to take the lead using the Six Cs.

# The Solution

# CHAPTER 7

# CONFLICT

## CASE STUDY

Andy Matheson is a 46-year-old operations director at a pharmaceutical company who thrives on change. Ambitious for the company to improve performance, he has a number of ideas as to how this might be achieved. Yet he voices none of them. Instead, in board meeting after board meeting, he finds himself passively watching his fellow directors playing out a game.

## Microcosm Moment

Today is no different. One director, Frank, is demolishing the enthusiasm and ideas of another director, Tony, by careful use of apparently unarguable logic and 'facts'. Juan, another director, expresses interest and support for both points of view. However, Andy knows this is nothing more than a charade. In reality, Juan seeks to prevent change in either direction so that neither Frank nor Tony 'wins'. This is because should one or other win, Juan would see himself as having 'lost'. He would, therefore, prefer to maintain the status quo even though he hates that too! So no one wins.

Andy has said very little, if anything, and now Richard, the CEO, is about to close the discussion by, as usual, postponing a decision until a later date. So yet again, nothing has been agreed and so nothing will change. The frustration this causes is discussed soon afterwards in dispersed huddles around the business. The overall effect is that everyone blames everyone else for the impasse.

This charade is one of many reasons why Andy has come to despise his colleagues including his boss, Richard. Worst of all he has come to despise himself for putting up with the situation and doing nothing.

What has happened here? Andy is rationalizing his behaviour by telling himself that nothing he can say or do will have any effect. Yet in his heart he knows that if he were to have the courage of his convictions and raise issues he wants to in meetings, he could count on enough support to make some changes.

All too often we find ourselves reluctant to speak up at important times at work. Sometimes, this may be when we are on the receiving end of games being played. Other times it may just be when we have new ideas or points of view that we want to convey to others. But we refrain from doing so.

Many of my clients feel misunderstood, undervalued or frustrated with the behaviour of others yet admit to sitting in meetings, appraisal, selection interviews, one-to-ones and not saying what's on their minds only to regret it later. Not only is this debilitating to the person, who is unable to be themselves at work, but also the equal tragedy is that work is losing half the person!

When I'm facilitating a group for, say, an hour's discussion, what I observe is one or two individuals who hold the floor with reasoned discussion, one or two others who argue their points aggressively and the majority watching in virtual silence. Those who remain silent may either look interested, vacant or incredulous. I have no idea what is going on in their minds since they are not speaking their minds. But my hunch is that whatever is going on internally would help the discussion change tack if they would give voice to it.

## SO WHERE'S THE CONFLICT?

My role in these group sessions is to reveal what team members are doing, why they are doing it and how each can handle comparable situations more resourcefully. I do so with the use of a conflict-handling model which illustrates well both the problems and the solutions (Thomas and Kilmann, 1974).

Why a conflict-handling model? Let's refer back to our case study. Imagine you are Andy and you are watching your fellow directors playing out the usual pretence. The following are some of your options with possible outcomes:

■ If you step in with an opinion on the item under discussion they may discount it – you have the potential for conflict
■ If you make an observation about the way two directors are arguing – you have potential for conflict directed at you by either of them

■ If you step in and ask for the discussion to move on because you've seen these two have similar arguments a million times – you have the potential for conflict with the other directors
■ If you say you'd like to take a short comfort break – you have potential for conflict
■ If you try and bring the conversation back to the original point on the agenda – you have potential for conflict
■ If you point out something that you know to be factually wrong – you have potential for conflict

It is extremely difficult for you to make an intervention in a group such as this without generating the potential for conflict. If an organization is encouraging creative problem solving, then by definition you are going to have people with different ideas, varying levels of attachment to their ideas and different modes of expressing this attachment.

Here's how a couple of clients explained their reaction to innocent suggestions by team members from other business functions:

I welcome new ideas, but most of the ones I hear are ill thought out and I tell my colleagues as much.

I have a specialism, it's my area of expertise and these people read a few pamphlets and suddenly they think they can do my job. Is it any wonder I belittle their contributions?

In this context, then, we can define conflict as a disagreement between two or more people.

## WHY DO WE AVOID CONFLICT?

One reason people avoid conflict is their perception of it. If you were to brainstorm words you associate with the word 'conflict', which is what I ask the teams with whom I work, you may well, like them, generate the following:

■ Anger
■ Aggression
■ War
■ Lose
■ Pain
■ Violence

- Divided
- Shouting
- Battle
- Fighting
- Frustration

What all these words have in common is that they are negative. If you now brainstorm all the positive words associated with conflict, you will more than likely choose some of the following:

- Problem Solving
- Resolution
- Solutions
- Collaboration
- Creativity
- Consensus
- Synergy
- Change
- Development
- Win–Win
- Peace

## WIN–WIN CULTURE

So, conflict is neither negative nor positive. The way in which conflict is experienced will depend on the way it is handled. When I ask teams how they could move from an experience of negative conflict characterized by list A to a positive debate characterized by list B they produce the central list shown in Table 7.1.

It is worth bearing in mind that change programmes promote a culture similar to that described in the right-hand, positive list B. This is a culture characterized by creative collaboration, participation and genuine team spirit in working together towards the same ends.

You may also recognize that the centre list of warrior-like interpersonal behaviours are those values our organizations urge us to live by.

Perceiving conflict as having positive outcomes when handled well is the first step to bridging the gap between the meeting culture and coffee machine culture. And to turning the coffee machine malcontents into the energized team players that our organization deserves.

First we need to understand how conflict is currently handled. The following model of conflict handling is not only a useful way of illus-

| Table 7.1 Bridging the gap between negative and positive conflict | | |
|---|---|---|
| **CONFLICT – From a Negative to a Positive Experience** | | |
| **LIST A: Negative Experience** | **WARRIOR-LIKE Behaviour** | **LIST B: Positive Experience** |
| ■ Anger <br> ■ Aggression <br> ■ War <br> ■ Lose <br> ■ Pain <br> ■ Violence <br> ■ Divided <br> ■ Shouting <br> ■ Battle <br> ■ Fighting <br> ■ Frustration | ■ Listen <br> ■ Ask questions <br> ■ Don't judge <br> ■ Discuss <br> ■ Be open <br> ■ Be considerate <br> ■ Be empathic <br> ■ Show respect <br> ■ Be objective <br> ■ Indulge <br> ■ Encourage | ■ Problem Solving <br> ■ Resolution <br> ■ Solutions <br> ■ Collaborate <br> ■ Creativity <br> ■ Consensus <br> ■ Synergy <br> ■ Change <br> ■ Development <br> ■ Win–Win <br> ■ Peace |

trating how perceptions of conflict impinge on the team's dynamics. It also provides alternative, more effective modes of operating within the team.

## CONFLICT-HANDLING MODEL

The Thomas–Kilmann Conflict Mode model (1974) suggests that we can handle conflict in two dimensions:

1. The horizontal 'cooperativeness' plane indicates the extent to which we are prepared to listen to and understand the other person's point of view.
2. The vertical 'assertiveness' plane indicates the extent to which we are prepared to have the courage to assert our own opinion and speak out.

The following is a description of each of the five types of conflict-handling styles (and see Figure 7.1):

*Top left-hand box:* People who operate out of this box are always asserting their own opinion but are not prepared to listen and cooperate with yours. We are described by team members as 'opinionated', 'bullies' or 'dictators'.

These people see conflict as having win–lose outcomes and will seek to argue in such a way that they win and you lose. In the model they are called *Competing*.

*Bottom right-hand box:* At the other end of the scale those who seek to cooperate with everyone else's opinion but do not

*Bottom left-hand box:*     assert their own are variously described as 'helpful', 'doormats' or 'wet' – especially by the competitive ones in the top left-hand box. These people tend to live with lose–win outcomes in conflict, with their losing and others winning. They are called *Accommodating*.

*Bottom left-hand box:*     Those who neither assert their own opinions nor participate in discussing the ideas of others, but instead stay silent, are frequently described as 'opting out', 'unhelpful' or 'withdrawn'. They contribute to conflict being experienced as lose–lose since their silent opinions can not be taken on board nor can those of the others' – not with team consensus, at any rate. They are called *Avoiding*.

*The centre box:*     Those who are happy to live with a compromise are described as 'half-hearted', 'generous' or 'malleable'. These settle for a draw and are called *Compromising*.

*The top right-hand box:* People who are prepared both to speak out and say what they think and listen to, and try to understand, the points of view of others are described as 'team leaders', 'democratic' or 'motivational'. People in this box seek win–win solutions and are called *Collaborating*.

## WHY OPERATE FROM THE LOWER TRIANGLE?

The times when we most often look for courage but do not find it are when someone is acting out of the competitive, left-hand box. Consequently, many of us spend much of our working life in the lower triangle. Figure 7.1 illustrates the five conflict-handling modes with the lower triangle.

You may recognize from your own experience of teamwork the following occurring:

- One or two people in competing mode, who want to win at the expense of other people's ideas and opinions
- One or two unsuccessfully attempting to collaborate with them
- The majority avoiding in silence or accommodating unconvincingly or seeking a compromise

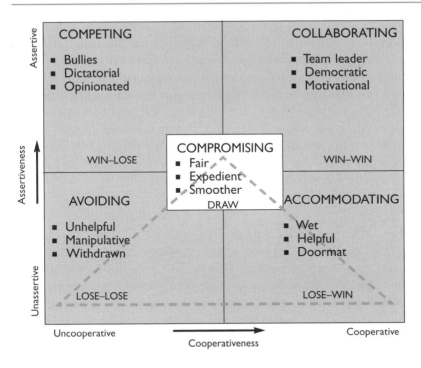

**Figure 7.1** The five conflict-handling modes

*Source:* Adapted from Thomas and Kilmann, 1974

The result is that apparent consensus decisions made at the end are in fact ones that have been imposed by a vocal minority.

No wonder then that when we take a break, the reaction to the most recent decision is one of uproar – outside the meeting room. A number of the team disagree vehemently. Nevertheless we have allowed the aggressive and assertive team members to dominate the meeting and hijack the purpose and direction of the team. The negative effects of such group dynamics reverberate long after the meeting has closed. They may become evident in the manner in which the decisions are implemented: badly, slowly or not at all.

When we accommodate, avoid or compromise against our will, we often do so 'for the sake of a quiet life'. In our minds this is a sensible course of action because it avoids unnecessary conflict. An example may be the person who returns to his desk to find a colleague is using his PC without having asked permission to do so. Instead of being able to retake his seat, the person is asked by the colleague if he can first complete the task on which he is working. About to assert his right to resume his own work, the person thinks it is unreasonable not to agree to the request and instead walks around the office until his colleague has finished.

A similar principle underlies Andy's behaviour in his meeting. Rather than confront his colleagues and suffer the argument that he presumes will ensue, he chooses to avoid this discomfort and sit out each meeting in silence.

This 'anything for peace' approach is a short-term expediency – in the long term it leads to anything but peace! If we persistently put other people's needs before our own, we lose and they win. In time, we begin to resent, even despise the other person, our job and eventually, our life.

Worst of all, we find ourselves lying awake at three o'clock in the morning, realizing we have now begun to despise ourselves. We ask ourselves, 'Why do I do it? Why do I put up with it? How could I be so stupid?' Yet later that very same day we carry on doing the 'right thing' by others and put ourselves second! We feel like a doormat. And we will continue to feel like this until we learn alternative modes of response.

This model provides a visual image for those of us who tend to experience the Gulliver Effect. When we remain in the bottom triangle we do not stand up and be counted for fear of hurting others or getting hurt ourselves. This triangle can characterize not only our relationships at work, but also those at home, with our family, with our children, any individual or group of individuals with whom we come into contact.

## WHAT IS THE DOWNSIDE OF THE LOWER TRIANGLE?

If we spend much of our life working from the bottom triangle, our ideas will never get taken on board. Perhaps we have our own idea of how best to run our team meetings. Or we have a vision of how our division could excel. Or we can see that if the board would just work more collaboratively we could please the City and all other stakeholders. But because we don't stick our heads above the parapet and make these points, our team, division or company loses. Nor do we get to use our true potential and really shine. This is decidedly a lose–win or a lose–lose way to live our lives.

If we are one of the silent majority it is likely that we will not be aware of the extent to which we are unwittingly colluding in our own discomfort.

We may have imagined that the triggers for feeling unfulfilled at work are the behaviour of other team members, a lack of strong leadership, the organization culture and so on. After seeing this model and recognizing our part in the process, happily the solution, though daunting, is clearly closer to home and therefore within reach.

Once we acknowledge responsibility for following our destiny we have a choice. Either we can choose not to change – or we can become a Warrior.

Which is the riskier alternative? Well, we must be aware that not using our potential, being misperceived and living a life of regret constitutes a huge risk in itself. And it is pretty stressful to boot! Doesn't the effect of that far outweigh the risk of upsetting the applecart in order to be ourselves?

## WHAT ARE THE RISKS OF SPEAKING OUT?

Some of the risks of speaking out are:

- We'll look stupid or will be made to look stupid
- People will lower their opinion of us
- Our idea or point will be ignored
- We'll damage key relationships
- We won't be able to express ourselves clearly
- We'll get into a fight that's uncomfortable
- We'll become part of the problem not the solution

The paradox is that, our silence guarantees that most of these things already apply. No one has a high opinion of someone who rarely speaks, our key relationships will be highly unsatisfactory and our point is already being ignored – never mind not expressing ourselves clearly, we're hardly expressing ourselves at all.

The upside of speaking out, therefore, far outweighs the downside. There is no real upside to remaining silent and giving in all your life. The real risk in life is not to take the best option – and being in the top triangle of the model is assuredly the best option.

## WHY IS THE TOP TRIANGLE THE BEST OPTION?

I mentioned in Chapter 6 on leadership that most of us had a teacher at school who inspired us and whom we still recall with affection. If we stopped to consider from which of the top three boxes they operated, the probability is that we'd say the right-hand, collaborative box.

Such a teacher would accept any answer as a valuable contribution even if it wasn't the one they sought. Because we were accorded respect and acceptance they, in turn, earned our respect and we felt safe to continue speaking up with answers. During our time with this teacher we felt as if we were developing our full potential. This type of environment exemplifies the preferred learning environment of OD programmes and is illustrated in Figure 7.2.

Compare this with the teacher who came out of the left-hand, competing box. If we put our hands up in their class and gave a wrong answer they would make us feel very small. The chances are that from that moment on we would not risk further embarrassment.

Organizations in which a similar type of leader predominates will not exploit people's potential because they are unwilling to take the risks required to develop it. According to the values of this leader we either agree with them and get it right in their eyes, or we are stupid.

If we facilitate a culture where everyone is prepared to speak their minds we reap the benefits of their collective realized potential. And for the individual, there is no longer a feeling of unfulfilment but rather one of achievement.

When Andy saw this model, he recognized his behaviour in the board meetings as primarily accommodating and avoiding. He'd known he was unhappy but couldn't, until now, articulate why. Now he realized that his

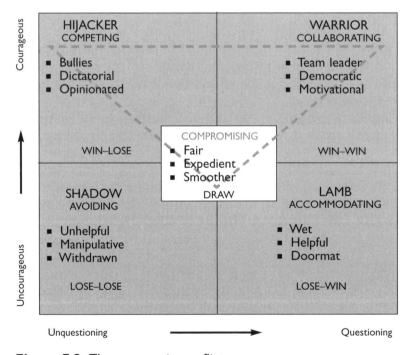

**Figure 7.2** The courage in conflict

*Source:* Adapted from Thomas and Kilmann, 1974

always giving in, so that he never got his own way, was the root cause of his unhappiness. His own behaviour was the cause of his feelings of frustration and powerlessness.

Previously Andy had blamed his colleagues for the team culture and silently speculated on how he could manage or change *their* behaviour. Now he realized that he had the power to change his situation by simply changing his own behaviour – finding the courage to make his point heard and deal with whatever results. Consequently, he felt energized, back in control. Now that he understood he had chosen how he responded to conflict in the team and could choose to respond differently, he no longer felt trapped by the egocentric behaviour of others.

## WE NEED TO BE VERSATILE

The real skill is to be able to select our mode of operating in conflict situations as appropriate. As we will see in the following chapter, we develop habitual styles of responding to conflict in groups very early on in life. If, as a child, we found that making ourselves scarce, remaining in our bedrooms quietly reading until things 'blew over' worked, then it is likely that as adults we will continue to behave as 'good boys' or 'good girls' when conflict is in the air and keep a low profile. If, on the other hand, as children we found that slamming doors, shouting and arguing worked, as adults we are likely to resort to this mode of behaviour when disagreements crop up.

Under stress, we do tend to revert to habitual forms of behaviour, even when they are clearly no longer of benefit to us. The skill is to have the versatility to select the appropriate behaviour. Competing is a reasonable response when dealing with a crisis. I always say that if, God forbid, my house was on fire and my two daughters were in it, I would not welcome the firefighters handling the situation from the top right-hand, collaborative box by asking me where I would like them to start!

In crisis situations you want leaders to be decisive. You want them to behave from the left-hand, competing box and say in effect – as I would expect from firefighters – no time for discussion, we're going in! Yet, it is worth noting that this style only works if the leader or colleague is collaborative for most of the time. In this case, they will have earned the respect and loyalty that will galvanize others to unquestioningly follow their lead when the situation calls for it. Otherwise they may encounter a less than adequate response.

Sometimes, because we have seen the same argument between team members over and over again with no solution, we may choose to avoid becoming embroiled it. Other times you are happy to accommodate others and let them have their way. At home we may want to go to the theatre but since our partner is set on the cinema we accommodate them. And compromise is an expected outcome of industrial relations disputes at work or negotiating the sale of our car or house.

The important thing is to know your own habitual form of behaviour and that of others and then, when needs be, have the courage to experiment with new modes of handling conflict in your life.

If we want to live in a world where we feel as comfortable as others do, it is vital we possess the courage to say what we believe and ask for what we want. This is equally relevant at work as it is with friends and family.

# CHAPTER 8

# CONCEPTS

## CASE STUDY

Gulliver found himself in a situation where they were speaking a foreign language. Consequently his understanding of what was going on around him was limited. In effect the foreign language is equivalent to the language of group dynamics for an inexperienced person. Without a 'language' for understanding the way people operate in groups, you may feel you have no idea where to start changing the way you are currently behaving in your team. The following is a case in point.

Mike Chambers, the senior partner of a brand consultancy, was having some difficulty working with one of his consultants, Kate Wyeth, during his team meetings. Although her manner was excellent with clients she was abrasive and offhand back in the office.

## Microcosm Moment

On this particular occasion, following a recent reorganization of the business function, Mike was expounding some ideas on how to imbed new working practices. However, as was often the case, at almost every suggestion he found that Kate either affected a negative expression or suggested his ideas were unworkable and did so in very uncompromising terms. Mike was pretty sure but couldn't be certain that Kate's latest bout of negativity was the result of his own disagreement with some ideas that she had during the last meeting.

Mike could see that Kate's behaviour was undermining his leadership of the team, but because he only had a hunch about her motives he did not know how to deal with it. He felt adrift.

If like Mike you have experienced this sense of powerlessness when neither reaching out nor giving as good as you get makes a difference, you will have wanted the tools to deal with the situation skilfully.

This chapter will show you how to acquire a framework of understanding so that you know what goes on in groups and can respond appropriately. There is no point in having an Inner Warrior if you either collude in ignorance or intervene clumsily. You will soon become part of the problem rather than influencing a solution.

## PERSONAL AND HIDDEN AGENDAS

In a business sense, when two or more people gather in a room, they will bring their personal agendas with them. Regardless of their willingness to be task focused, these agendas will become a problem if not managed properly.

Personal agendas include expectations of what a successful meeting constitutes. Most people will expect there to be a leader, some form of agenda, that everyone arrives on time and so on.

They will also be keen to ensure that they achieve certain things in the context of their own and others' performance. These will include getting from others the recognition for positive contributions they make, attaining a realistic level of power and/or control and so on.

Everyone has a personal agenda but, like Kate's, sometimes elements of this agenda will be hidden.

The personal agenda of an MD of a business unit may be to get more leads from the marketing director. This can be expressed as a simple polite request followed by a cooperative discussion. If, however, he has an additional aim of making the marketing director look incompetent in the eyes of their boss, this represents his hidden agenda which he will articulate through negative body language and comments.

If hidden agendas aren't managed skilfully they will make everyone observing feel uncomfortable and disrupt the group. The atmosphere they create is not conducive to effective group interaction. Indeed the rest of the team sits frozen not knowing what to do and resentful that the leader has been fooled. The result is they don't use their energy to confront what has happened, nor do they use it on the next item of the agenda. They are effectively no longer 'present' in the meeting that was first called. Now they are at a completely different meeting – one that they want to get out of as quickly as possible.

Only when they are back in corridor get-togethers will they once again burst with energy. They feel they can speak freely amongst like-minded colleagues and be authentic.

We can see then that people who stay silent in the face of games being played out in groups are not being authentic nor are those who themselves play the games as part of their hidden agendas. So with the possible exception of the leader who takes events at face value, hidden agendas are responsible for everyone in the meeting being inauthentic.

## GROUPS ARE A PROBLEM WAITING TO HAPPEN

You may now recognize that you are avoiding, accommodating or compromising. And you may want to be more assertive and work from the top triangle of the conflict-handling model. But as you look around the group there are so many interactions taking place that you do not know where, how or when to begin. Understanding group dynamics can be daunting by virtue of the sheer number of relationships involved.

As Michael Kindred (1987) puts it, in a family of three you may have the following relationships:

- Mother and father
- Mother and child
- Father and child

If another child is born into the family, the number of relationships increases dramatically:

- Mother and father
- Mother and older child
- Mother and younger child
- Father and older child
- Father and younger child
- Older child and younger child

Add one to a group of three and you've doubled the number of relationships with which members have to deal.

If you want to work out how many relationships are going on in your team, do the following sum (the answer might surprise you):

$$\frac{\text{(number in group)} \times \text{(number in group less one)}}{2}$$

For example, for a team of 10, the number of relationships is:

$$\frac{10 \times 9}{2} = 45$$

But this is no reason for avoiding the significance of process issues in either accomplishing or falling short of the task.

## OUR FIRST HUMAN GROUP

We all start in our lives as authentic people but it is our early experiences of group dynamics that transform our behaviour. Recently, I was watching a family walking along the Thames towpath. I observed the three-year-old son happily bobbing along next to his mother. A little further ahead, I observed the father with his head down, his hands dug into his pockets followed several steps behind by his six-year-old son walking in a similar fashion.

It was clear that the two children had responded in very different ways to a disagreement that had taken place between their parents. Nothing could break the self-confidence felt by the three-year-old. By contrast his older brother looked uneasy. His father appeared to be feeling annoyed by the mother. The child understood this and was already accommodating his father's threatening mood by keeping a low profile for fear of being the butt of his anger.

Sadly nobody can live in a bubble. The three year old will become aware of the dynamics of the family just as his brother has. He, being the younger child may, however, learn to deal with his father's mood by fearlessly nagging until he gets his own way. This learning in our first human group is a precursor to what happens in groups in organizations. By the time we enter them, we've all learnt our default methods of dealing with atmospheres.

## MANAGING A GROUP EFFECTIVELY

The result of our inauthenticity in human groups – including a group of just two – is that we suffer from the Gulliver Effect – we behave as Lambs and Shadows rather than the Warriors we once were. This means that any advantages of working in groups, such as wealth of knowledge, multiplicity of approaches, enhanced commitment to allocated tasks and reduced communication problems, will be minimized.

Bringing hidden agendas and ego-defensive behaviour to the fore and dealing with them is a prerequisite of successful teamwork. Otherwise, teamwork can become a major liability to an organization's success.

The effects of unsuccessful group work include:

- Conforming under pressure
- A free hand given to dominant individuals
- Silence taken for agreement
- Successful pursuit of hidden agendas
- Time constraints used to limit in-depth or democratic debate
- Inadequate management of disagreements
- Premature discussion of solutions
- Conflicting goals and objectives
- Insensitivity to feelings
- Revenge cycles
- Opting out
- A paucity of creative contributions
- Poor decisions with minimal commitment
- Idiosyncratic implementation of decisions

## WHY DON'T PEOPLE ADDRESS PROCESS ISSUES?

Whilst this is happening, rather than raise the real issues, people instead keep their heads down below the parapet, and politely sit the meeting out. Why don't people address these process issues? Because they think they'll go away if you push hard enough with the task. This is what my clients tell me when I ask them. My response to them is to ask, 'Have you ever gone home, walked in the house and realized that your partner is unhappy about something, then ignored it in the hope it will go away? Has it, in fact, ever gone away?' Invariably they laugh and say 'No'. Then I ask them 'What does happen?' They answer that it either remains an issue hanging between them as an atmosphere or more likely the situation deteriorates. But it never goes away.

Everyone has the same argument with their partner throughout the time they are together. The content may differ; one week it may be which shade of paint to decorate the wall, another week it may be where to spend their holiday and another which school to send their children. But the underlying issues remain the same. Maybe one partner feels their views are not respected by the other or perhaps another feels they are coopted too often into doing things they don't want to do or one feels that they are the one who always give in. The point is that settling on pink or blue for the wall, Maldives or Prague for the holiday or public or private school does not solve the underlying problem. The reason the arguments reoccur is because underlying resentments and built-up hurt – the process issues – remain untouched. We argue to defend our ego not to defend our stance on the issue at hand.

What makes us think different rules apply at work? Once we have been persuaded that we cannot afford to avoid process issues, we will want to learn how to recognize and deal with them. A deeper understanding of personal and interpersonal behaviour helps individuals take a more active and self-conscious role in their social and work life. The following are some observation guidelines to help process analyse group behaviour.

## SENSING THE SITUATION

When a discussion seems to be going nowhere or tension is in the air or an intellectualized conflict is clearly obscuring a personal one, we can guaranteed that a hidden agenda is lying just beneath the surface. An effective tool to sense where this hidden conflict lies is that of the four focal issues developed by Blake and Mouton (1983). It is worth asking which of the following process issues is at large:

1. *Power and control* – people are competing for dominance or leadership.
2. *Norms and standards* – people disagree both about the nature of rules, processes or procedures and the degree to which they have to observe them.
3. *Goals and objectives* – people are focusing on diverse goals and objectives.
4. *Morale and cohesion* – bad feelings (perhaps created by conflict around the other three focal issues) are having a corrosive effect on energy levels and motivation.

A conversation between a sales director and the finance director regarding the use of a database may mask an underlying focal issue of 'norms and standards'. Everyone senses the hidden agenda (which is to attack the other's values and attitudes about following rules and procedures), but because it is unspoken it never becomes the topic of discussion. Their argument about the database goes nowhere because it is their lack of respect for each other's approach that is the real focus of their conflict. The sales director thinks the finance director is picky and overcontrolling, the finance director is disturbed by the sales director's maverick approach to documentation and detail. This is illustrated in Table 8.1 along with the differences they have on the other three focal issues.

If Gulliver had a flipchart with these four focal issues on it and asked, Which of these four is going on in the group right now? they would have agreed it was an issue of power and control. Every conversation about any topic would have an underlying dynamic of threat, resentment and compe-

| | Finance director (ST)<br>Preference | Sales director (NF)<br>Preference |
|---|---|---|
| Norms and standards | ■ Obedience to rules and procedures control, following orders, rigidity, risk aversion | ■ Casual approach to rules and procedures, autonomy, entrepreneurship, flexibility, creative risk taking |
| Power and authority | ■ We'll do it our leader's way | ■ We'll do it my way |
| Goals and objectives | ■ Productivity, work flow, gross profit, a tightly run 'ship', methodical | ■ Personal relationships, net profit, commission, expediency, fun |
| Morale and cohesion | ■ Irrelevant to task achievement | ■ Central to task achievement |

**Table 8.1** Focal issues in team meetings

tition. Having raised the underlying focal issues, he could then deal with it. He might say, 'I'm not a threat to you. I simply want to stand up and be free, as you are.'

When there is little team spirit or collaboration, one of the four focal issues will be at play. This model provides a common language with which to illustrate the group dynamics and move forward to some collaborative agreement.

## UNDERSTANDING GROUP BEHAVIOUR

When we sense an atmosphere in our group for whatever reason, asking ourselves the following questions will provide a map of the group dynamics. The group dynamics will be the sum total of each individual's contribution.

## Participation

- *Hijackers:* Who are the high participators? Who talks to whom? Is there any reason for this?
- *Lambs:* Who are the low participators? How are the quieter people treated? Do some people move in and out of the group, for example lean forward or backward? When do they come in with a contribution or opt out?
- *Shadows:* Is silence interpreted as consent, disdain, manipulation or indifference?
- *Warriors:* Who keeps the ball rolling? Why?

## Listening

- *Hijackers:* Who cuts off others or interrupts them?
- *Lambs:* Who helps others get into the discussion?
- *Shadows:* Are some members preoccupied and not listening?
- *Warriors:* Are there any attempts to help others clarify their ideas?

## Bids for Power and Control

- *Hijackers:* Is there rivalry for power and control? How does it influence the other group members?
- *Lambs:* Who are uninfluential such that people neither listen to them nor follow their lead?
- *Shadows:* Do some members seem to be outsiders and others insiders? How are outsiders treated?
- *Warriors:* Who are influential, in that people listen to and follow their lead?

## Style of Influence

- *Hijackers:* Does anyone try to take control of the meeting and have it run their way? Who clashes most sharply with others during the meeting? Does anyone block action or pass judgement on other group members when things are not going in their direction?
- *Lambs:* Is anyone consistently deferential to other group members? Do any members avoid saying anything negative? Who is most ready to support others?
- *Shadows:* Does anyone appear to go along with group decisions without seeming to commit themselves one way or another? Who seems to be withdrawn from or psychologically opted out of the meeting? Who does not initiate activity, participates mechanically or only responds when asked?
- *Warriors:* Does anyone try to include everyone in the discussion? Who expresses their ideas and feelings openly and directly without judging others? Who is open to and welcomes feedback?

## Quality of Decision Making

- *Hijacker:* Does anyone make a decision and attempt to move on without checking it out with everyone? Can you see any reason for this? What effect does this have on the other group members?
- *Lambs:* Does the group drift from topic to topic without ever coming to

a decision? Who supports others' suggestions no matter what? How does this 'pairing' affect other group members?

- *Shadows:* Is there evidence of a vocal minority pushing for a decision over others' silent objections? Does anyone attempt to make a contribution that does not receive recognition or a response? What effect does this have on the person?
- *Warriors:* Who attempts to get everyone involved in a consensus decision?

## Handling and Use of Conflict

- *Hijackers:* Who prefers an atmosphere of conflict and disagreement? Do certain members provoke or annoy others? How do members react when their ideas are not accepted?
- *Lambs:* Who prefers a congenial atmosphere? Is there an attempt to suppress conflict?
- *Shadows:* Who tries to avoid conflict or an unpleasant atmosphere? Who prefers an atmosphere of covert discontent?
- *Warriors:* When conflict arises, who is willing to deal with it in an objective manner? Who prefers a friendly atmosphere? Is the atmosphere one of play, competition, work, taking flight, frustration and so on?

## Sensitivity to Feelings

- *Hijackers:* How well is the group able to deal with emotional as well as intellectual conflicts? Are group members aware of the interpersonal issues that get in the way of their working together? Do they attempt to resolve the situation?
- *Lambs:* Do members attempt to support others when they reject their ideas? How sensitive to feelings are group members? How do they get raised or suppressed? By whom?
- *Shadows:* Do people feel free to express feelings and emotions?
- *Warriors:* Does the group get beneath surface issues in discussions?

## Group Norms

- *Hijackers:* Are certain areas avoided in the group, such as challenging personal agendas or leadership?
- *Lambs:* Do people agree with each other too readily? Do conversations tend to be restricted to work-related topics or events outside the group?
- *Shadows:* Are people involved and interested?

- *Warriors:* What happens when members disagree?

The above questions can help raise awareness of the everyday dynamics we encounter in our working groups. This is illustrated in Figure 8.1.

The following headings are useful terms to use when raising and dealing with these dysfunctional group dynamics.

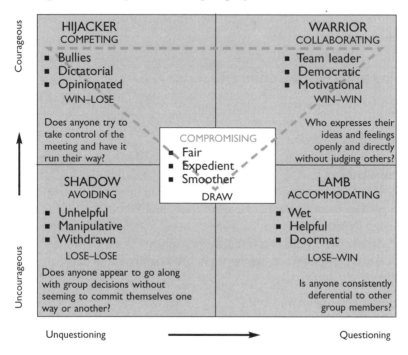

**Figure 8.1** Referencing dysfunctional behaviours in groups

*Source:* Adapted from Thomas and Kilmann, 1974

## KNOWING YOURSELF/KNOWING OTHERS

*Ground rules:* All groups – families, work, and social – have their ground rules or group norms, often not stated, but nevertheless very powerful in controlling group behaviour. Such rules include the extent to which you can disagree with team members, who does most of the talking and how decisions are taken. Making your ground rules – your group values – explicit is a useful tool with which members can confront inappropriate behaviour without it being seen to be making a personal attack. A five-minute process review at the end of each meetings would result in Hijackers feeling less able to hijack meetings and Lambs and Shadows feeling able to speak up.

*Punctuality:* Certain people are known to habitually arrive late. This can not only be frustrating for those kept waiting but it also sends out a signal that the latecomer has little respect for the meeting. Yet we rarely raise timekeeping as an issue, preferring to sidestep it with a joke or sarcastic comment. Similarly, finishing on time is no less important. For most people, meetings which go on past their allotted finishing time are extremely annoying. Starting and finishing meetings on time helps to prevent the process issues of tuning out, revenge cycles, reduced attendance and walkouts.

*Jealousy:* Jealousy is a major influence on group dynamics and epitomizes sibling rivalry. When we are jealous, we feel resentful because we fear our status, power and inclusion within the group are being subverted by another group member. One group member, at that moment, is more popular and powerful in the eyes of our leader and colleagues than we are and this threatens our own popularity and capacity to influence within the group. We may not always be aware of it but it lies behind rational debate being abandoned in favour of ego-driven debate.

My client Cheryl Austin attended a residential Strategic Offsite. During the two days, she experienced considerable frustration due to a feeling that her contributions were not being accorded the respect they deserved. At the same time, she was aware that contributions from another woman, Joanna, were receiving a more sympathetic ear from their boss. She also felt resentment because of the influence in shaping the group's discussion this gave her. As a result Cheryl seemingly could not stop herself irrationally and aggressively dismissing everything Joanna said.

Others of us will respond to jealousy by being silent in the meeting and voluble outside it.

*Bids for leadership:* If a person is allowed to dominate a group, the leader may lose cooperation from other group members and eventually the dominant person may, in effect, take over the leadership. If leaders do not establish their authority from the start, they are likely to face a challenge from one or more of the group who are especially keen to advance their interests. A rebellion by the others may result in some sulkily becoming Shadows, some politely being Lambs whilst others mirror the Hijackers in a counterbid for leadership.

*Playing politics:* Playing politics has been defined as substituting rational, data-based decisions with influence through power. By using statements designed to appeal to logic (whilst avoiding acknowledging that logic is not the same as rationality), as power brokers we attempt to bring about a solution that maintains our power without responding to our colleagues' or our organization's needs. This is a poor alternative to finding a rational, justifiable basis for goal setting and operational activities. One way to replace politics with rationality is to confront hidden agendas.

*Clarity of objectives:* Often teams will launch into the first item on the agenda, only to find 25 minutes in, that they lack direction and do not have a common understanding of the purpose of the discussion. Sometimes there is not even a common understanding of the purpose of the meeting. This will generate discontent in the team which may or may not be raised. In the latter case, people may either withdraw from the discussion or continue the discussion but in a disagreeable manner.

*Pairing and subgroups:* One block against cohesion in the group is the establishment of pairs. We feel more powerful inside a pair than alone. What tends to happen is that two people (or more) start sitting together at meetings and exchange nods, agree with anything the other says or whisper confidences. It's as if they have entered into an unwritten contract that they won't disagree with one another. This can make us feel jealous and left out.

Because we want to be included but are excluded, we create our own subgroup and our own sense of power. The group ethos is then lost because every time one subgroup says one thing the other tends to say the opposite. The result is that a consensus is rarely if ever achieved.

An IT Executive, Brian Markham recalls: 'I was in a team where every time one person said something, their pal would agree with them. And when this happened, one of the members of the rival pair would disagree only to be supported by his pal. The rest of us looking on colluded with this impasse by inwardly supporting one camp or the other, even though we equally were frustrated by the lack of progress that this game of wills caused. Nothing was said during the meeting but when we broke for coffee, all hell broke loose. Two camps would huddle together and discuss what kept taking place but no one ever raised it in the real meeting.'

*Remaining silent:* We sometimes fear speaking out in a meeting because we don't want to be seen as stupid. We don't have sufficient confidence in our experience or we expect others to know what we know anyway. The paradox is that by not speaking out for fear of looking stupid we look stupid for not speaking out – for the entire meeting!

*Style of influence:* Levels of desire to exert power, influence and control vary. Some people prefer formal channels when adding items to the agenda, others will find ways to exert an influence upon the way things develop less overtly such as building relationships outside the meeting. Some talk often and noisily. But everyone has an investment in pushing things in a certain direction.

*Scapegoating:* Problems experienced by team members are sometimes projected onto a colleague, who becomes a 'scapegoat'. Several team members will have a sense of relief that another member has shown the courage to express anxiety or difficulty that they too are experiencing. Rather than admit to this, they focus the discussion on solving their colleague's problem so as to take the spotlight off their own.

Another form of scapegoating is to blame someone or some body *outside* the team such as another function or leader. A competent leader will be aware that focusing on the 'there and then' rather than the 'here and now' is 'running away' and will bring the focus of attention back into the group where the problems lie.

*Opting out:* Some people may become so anxious by what is happening in a group that they will find ways of opting out. They may remain unusually silent for long periods, daydream or move their chair slightly back out of the group. It has association with the notion of passive–aggressive sulkiness and is difficult to challenge since the person is doing nothing inappropriate and so often gets away with it.

*Use of body language:* Much communication in a group is of the non-verbal kind. A great deal of what we communicate to others is done through facial expression, posture, tone of voice, speed of delivery, direct or indirect eye contact, gestures of the hand and blushing – the non-verbal signals being relayed across the room that are often most revealing. A secret glance, wink or look of incredulity speaks far louder than words.

*Red herrings and humour as avoidance:* Due to feelings of anxiety, enthusiasm or rebelliousness team members may deflect others from the task in hand. An example of a red herring is an anecdote we suddenly feel compelled to tell. On other occasions, the group generates humour to shift attention away from the task at hand or from process issues.

*Selective perception:* If what is being asked of them creates a high level of anxiety, individuals may, rather than attempt the task and fail or confront themselves and their fears, conduct themselves with an apparent understanding of what is required, only to later show innocent surprise at having done something else. A rebellious group or subgroup can easily evade the real task by so literally interpreting a request as to make the activity unworkable or a disaster. A frequent accompaniment is then to blame the leader for giving ambiguous instructions.

*Blocking:* One of the commonest causes of poor group performance is due to members who block others. Almost everyone has experienced being in a group with a persistent 'blocker' who always, no matter what the suggestion, has to raise objections without having any concrete suggestions of his or her own. Blocking suggestions can inhibit those who are prepared to offer their thoughts and ideas to the group and limit the range of ideas from which the group has to choose.

*Interrupting or shutting out:* Interrupting others, or shutting them out, will ensure that their contribution is given the least attention. Over-talking, dismissing what has been said, making light of it, and exaggerating it to make the idea or the person appear ridiculous are all methods of shutting out, and have the effect of reducing trust and openness. Disagreement and controversy are important, but how disagreements are stated and how controversy is conducted can be productive or damaging to group performance.

*Hearing versus listening:* Most people do not really 'listen' when others are talking; they are too busy preparing what it is they have to say and looking for an opportunity to say it. They are also evaluating what they hear and making judgements about how it fits in with their own assessment. They are hearing the words rather than really listening. It goes something like this – receive what you say/critically judge it/prepare my reply.

*Point scoring:* If you are feeling somewhat at a disadvantage in a team for some reason, one way of trying to cope with it is to do or say something which puts another member (or members) at a disadvantage. For example, someone may have disagreed with something you said. You then wait for a chance to disagree with them. This game of point scoring is called a *revenge cycle.* Unless it is acknowledged and talked about, it can disrupt the real task of the team.

*Interruptions:* Another unwelcome signal is when members of the team leave to answer a phone call or enquiry, go to the toilet, or simply stand up to get themselves a coffee. Unless stated otherwise, such interruptions suggest these people are not really interested in the current discussion, their colleagues or the meeting in general.

*Endings:* There are occasions when there is too much 'unfinished business' around to allow for a comfortable end to the meeting.

A may still be seething at something B said
C may be feeling hurt by a remark made by D last week
E may not have recovered from being made the group casualty
F may feel that she has missed taking over the leadership
G may be annoyed with B for getting at A
H may be the only one free of tangles and can't understand why people look so miserable. (after Michael Kindred, 1987)

The situation needs careful handling. A leader who senses the atmosphere could fall into the trap of beginning the meeting all over again, so to speak, annoying those who wish to leave on time. A leader who ignores or is insensitive to the atmosphere may happily close the meeting only to be shocked when few actions have been implemented by the following meeting.

## EFFECTIVE GROUP PARTICIPATION

In all human interactions there are two major ingredients – content and process. As we saw in Chapter 5, the first deals with the subject matter or the task upon which the group is working. In most interactions, the focus of attention of all persons is on the content.

The second ingredient, process, is concerned with what is happening between and to group members while the group is working. Group process, or dynamics, deals with such items as morale, sensitivity to feelings, atmosphere, participation, styles of influence, leadership struggles, conflict, competition, cooperation, and so on.

We all have different needs which we seek to satisfy via membership of the team, whether they are a need for attention, to win, to feel included, to achieve, for approval or to feel safe. The balance of all the different individual needs helps to produce the distinctive style and climate of the group and explains how different teams have different 'personalities'. The combination leads to different teams displaying different characteristic ways of relating together. In most interactions, very little attention is paid to process, even when it is the major cause of ineffective group action.

Sensitivity to group process will better enable us to diagnose group problems early and deal with them more effectively. Since these processes are present in all groups, awareness of them will enhance a person's worth to a group and enable him or her to be a more effective group participant.

So what of Mike, our baffled senior partner? How does he confront Kate with his suspicions? The answer is for the group to draw up ground rules, which might include: 'raising issues as they arise', 'confronting personal agendas' and 'no revenge cycles'. Mike could turn to these laminated values on the wall and ask Kate whether she thought they were getting into a revenge cycle. He could then explain what he meant and they would begin a dialogue that would go from content, to process, and back to content again. This is very risky and it does require courage, but you cannot solve a problem unless it is on the table. Understanding group behaviours and how to raise and resolve them is vital if we're to begin to eliminate the Gulliver Effect. Developing the confidence to do so is the subject of the next chapter.

# CHAPTER 9

# COLLABORATION

## CASE STUDY

Susan Maitland is an HR manager for a large clothing firm. She loves what she does and is passionate about the people she serves. Very often she has an instinct for the right course of action. Her boss is Edward Brooks, who brings an intellectual approach to his work and projects an intimidating figure. Though Edward recognizes and respects Susan's ability he wants a malleable 'child' reporting directly to him. He achieves this by subtly undermining her confidence. He employs diversionary tactics which she, instead of challenging, either ignores or tolerates.

## Microcosm Moment

Susan has been asked by Edward about progress in filling a vacancy. Susan replies that a person has been found who has sailed through the assessment centre and is now set to be recruited. She goes on to enthusiastically outline the reasons why this candidate would be a good fit for the position. Yet, instead of complimenting her on finding a suitable candidate, Edward immediately asks the pointless question: 'What is your contingency plan?'

Susan knows all too well this question is designed to undermine her confidence. It is a tactic familiar to her. Nevertheless, the effect on her is one of deflation. She goes red and tries to bluff her way out of the situation, because she does not have an answer.

Once again, Edward has succeeded in his game of one-upmanship. But, although he has won another of the battles he feels he needs to fight, he ultimately won't win the war. The war is to preserve his position and status. He won't win it because by undermining an important colleague the business will suffer and this will eventually rebound on him.

Susan's response to the pressure that Edward is exerting is to either accommodate or avoid. In the microcosm moment, she chooses to take his question at face value and removes herself from the fray, rather than challenge Edward on his hidden agenda. This tactic began to take its toll and Susan came to see me because she was losing her confidence as a competent professional and hence, the ability to perform in her role.

I used the conflict-handling model to illustrate what was going on between herself and her boss. When Edward was being a Hijacker, acting from the competing box, she habitually went into the bottom triangle and acted either as a Shadow, avoiding conflict or a Lamb by being accommodating.

If the situation between herself and Edward was ever to be resolved she knew she would have to tap back into her Inner Warrior and so find the courage she will need to get into the collaborative box. Then she can raise the real issues – that of Edward's bid for power and control and the impact of his influencing style – with the confidence she once enjoyed.

She then asked me, as so many clients do, How exactly do I do that? The following model, based on *transactional analysis* (TA), is a useful place to start.

## OUR FOUR LIFE POSITIONS

There are four life positions that we can find ourselves in at any one time. You may not realize it but you have probably been in three of them several times today. The fourth is a position that in an ideal world none of us would be in, but unfortunately many of us are.

At any given moment in life, we feel either good about ourselves or bad. We might feel good, for example, when we have worked hard to complete a task and are satisfied we have done the best we could do. By contrast, if we have rushed to complete the task and know we have not given of our best, we will feel bad. This bad feeling will be brought into sharp focus when another person sees the fruits of our labour.

The same principle applies to how we feel about other people. If we have received warm and genuine praise from somebody, we will feel good about them. If, on the other hand, we have been mismanaged or treated shoddily, we will feel bad about that person.

This leads to four combinations that make up the life positions in which we can find ourselves as shown in Figure 9.1.

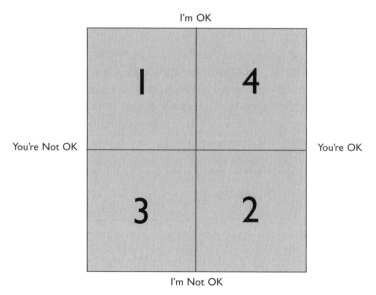

I'm OK

You're Not OK

You're OK

I'm Not OK

**Figure 9.1** The four life positions

1. If you feel good about yourself but bad about somebody else you are in I'm OK – You're Not OK, the top left-hand box.
2. If you feel bad about yourself but good about somebody else you are in I'm Not OK – You're OK, the bottom right-hand box.
3. If you feel bad about yourself and bad about somebody else you are in I'm Not OK – You're Not OK, the bottom left-hand box.
4. If you feel good about yourself and good about somebody else you are in I'm OK – You're OK, the top right-hand box.

## I. I'm OK –You're Not OK

Let us imagine you are standing in a bar talking to someone about country-side issues and they say contemptuously, 'I can't believe you don't support fox hunting.' Or you say to your teenage daughter or son, 'I can't believe you can live in a bedroom like this.'

When one person is speaking to another in this way, they are in 'I'm OK – You're Not OK' mode. This means they are going for a 'win' for them and 'lose' for the other person.

Why do people behave this way? The aggression that these people project may make them seem strong and confident and that they are OK but in reality this is a façade. In fact, they are feeling more Not OK about themselves than they are about you.

So although their behaviour belies it, they are psychologically coming out of Box 2, which is I'm Not OK – You're OK. In order to defend their ego they take an aggressive stance.

## 2. I'm Not OK – You're OK

Imagine you are about to go into a job interview and from inside the room you hear laughter as the panel says goodbye to the first candidate. You immediately think, 'They obviously like her. I'll never convince them to take me.' The daunting task ahead strikes fear into your heart. You then start to convince yourself that nothing you have prepared is adequate – not the suit you are wearing nor your knowledge of the company nor the questions you had planned to ask.

At this moment you are in I'm Not OK – You're OK. By the time you finally walk into the interview room, when one of the panel asks you your name your mind goes completely blank! If your anxiety endures, you lose and they win. You lose because you give a poor interview and don't get the job. They win because they hire the 'right' candidate instead.

## 3. I'm Not OK – You're Not OK

This is a relatively unhealthy mode. There are four main types of individual who frequent this life position:

- the tortured adolescent who feels bad about themselves, school, their parents and the world. So they spend much of their time sitting alone in a darkened room listening to music
- the depressed person who feels powerless and that life is pointless
- the person who is momentarily in this box, say after a divorce, redundancy or failed business venture, yet like Van Gogh or Nietzsche will find creativity by plumbing the depths of their despair
- the person who should be avoided as far as is humanly possible! They always have a reason why they cannot do what you ask of them now. No matter how much you try to make friends with them they are always cold the next time you meet them. They hate themselves and everyone else and the only way they can feel 'up' is to drag everyone else down into their I'm Not OK – You're Not OK box.

Those who habitually come out of this box are difficult to work or live with. This is the passive–aggressive personality that I described in Chapter 2. While you are speaking to them you assume they are taking on board what you are saying and are in collaborative mode. But either they have no intention of doing what is asked of them – or they will do it in their own time in their own way.

You cannot win with people when they are in this life position and they can't win either. This is lose–lose.

# 4. I'm OK –You're OK

Have you ever been for a job that you didn't really want and got it anyway? If so, you were likely to be in box 4. You were relaxed, able to improvise easily and this in turn made the interviewers relaxed and warm to you. You came across as both interested and interesting.

This is win–win. You win because you get the job – or at least have the choice of taking the job. The interviewers win because they get what they believe is the best candidate.

This is the most constructive position. We accept our own worth and that of others. People here are happy, productive, energetic and at peace with themselves. Wouldn't it be great if we could stay in this box for the rest of our lives?

When we behave in this manner, I'm OK – You're OK, we are sensitive to other people's needs and wants, do not take poor behaviour or language personally and achieve a rational, objective dialogue. We do not allow our ego to impair our ability to generate ideas and be creative nor cloud our judgement of the contributions of others. This, therefore, is the preferred box for collaborative problem solving.

## FEEL COLLABORATIVE!

Now that we understand these four life positions and their meaning, we are ready to answer Susan's original question: How do I stay in the collaborative box?

If we superimpose the four boxes on to the conflict-handling model, we can see that when we are:

■ Competing, we are feeling I'm OK – You're Not OK
■ Accommodating, we are feeling I'm Not OK – You're OK
■ Avoiding, we are feeling I'm Not OK – You're Not OK
■ Collaborating, we're feeling I'm OK – You're OK

The result is a robust framework for understanding and interpreting what we are *feeling* in any given conflict situation. With an understanding of what is healthy and what is not, we are able to select the right option (see Figure 9.2).

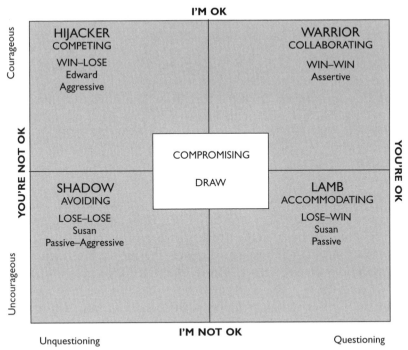

**Figure 9.2** Relationship between conflict-handling styles and the four life positions

*Source:* Adapted from Thomas and Kilmann, 1974

The right option will depend on a number of variables such as:

- The individual you are working with
- The situation you find yourself in
- Your preferred styles

As I pointed out in Chapter 7 on conflict, there will be instances when staying in the collaborative box is not the right option. Sometimes it is better to avoid conflict, for example when an issue is trivial and other more important issues are pressing. Other times it will be prudent to meet aggression head on, such as when somebody tries to bully you (since bullies admire bullies). Other times still, when you want to be generous you will happily accommodate, compromise or avoid conflict.

The point is that the difference between doing this before learning the framework and doing it after, is that before, you habitually 'jump into a box' with a heavy heart – as a reflexive response to the situation you find yourself in. The real skill is to select the appropriate option. If we are connected to our Inner Warrior, we feel OK about ourselves and others, and have the confidence to choose, calmly and rationally how we will respond.

Returning to Susan, we can see that in her dealing with Edward's aggression she tends to occupy two of the boxes – accommodating and avoiding – but not of her own volition. The decision is made for her unconsciously because she has not yet learnt to behave as a Warrior. Were she a Warrior she would be making a conscious choice.

When Edward projects from the I'm OK – You're Not OK box and tries to wrong-foot her, she immediately goes into the I'm Not OK – You're OK box. She gets flustered, her heart speeds up. She suddenly feels small; while Edward takes on the appearance of a giant. Her mind races and she becomes tongue-tied. Eventually she answers, but poorly. Her discomfort makes her agree to anything he demands and passively accommodate him. The result is that not only does she feel disparaged, but also pointless extra work has been created for her. Both detract from Susan's enjoyment of her job and her effectiveness in carrying it out.

There is a danger that if Susan carries on in this mode of interaction she will move into I'm Not OK – You're Not OK. This life position is normally expressed by passive–aggressive resistance, something which is characterized by not willingly doing what's asked of you, yet neither saying you won't nor offering an alternative. By adopting a permanently sulky demeanour, life begins to feel pointless and very lose–lose – for both sides. It will eventually render Susan incapable of working effectively and possibly lead to ill health and depression.

## WHAT IS SUSAN DOING?

Let's imagine that the communication between Susan and Edward is realized in the form of light beams. When they interact, they shine a torch at one another. What does Susan do with the light from Edward's torch?

# Absorbing (I'm Not OK – You're OK)

When Susan is confronted by Edward's tone of voice and the insinuation that she has not fully completed the task her reaction is to absorb his light. In doing so, she allows herself to be blinded by it. The result it, she cannot now see clearly and she is unable to rebut what is a spurious question.

When we are absorbing someone else's light, we are in no position to fight or meet any kind of challenge. If we are accused of something, we will take it personally.

## Deflecting (I'm OK – You're Not OK)

But Susan is not always as flustered around Edward as on this occasion. She does not allow herself to be intimidated in meetings with others who see Edward for what he is – a Hijacker with a hidden agenda to exert power and take control. Instead of absorbing his light she deflects it. Rather than give in, she goes on the offensive. She still feels bad but rather than defer she responds aggressively in kind with put-downs to make him look and feel bad too.

When we are deflecting someone else's light, we think we are acting like a Warrior: standing up for our rights and those of others. But we are behaving like a Hijacker: taking things personally and attacking the person back. This kind of personal attack usually triggers a revenge cycle.

## Diffracting (I'm Not OK – You're Not OK)

When Edward puts her down sufficiently, she feels very unappreciated and this stance is expressed through passive–aggressive resistance. In respect of the new recruit, she will produce a contingency plan, but do so half-heartedly and with no real commitment. So Edward's light is bent out of shape when it is returned, revealing Susan's discontent. Susan is diffracting the light she receives.

If we spend our whole life attempting to make other people feel as bad as we feel, no one wins. If, for spite, we do our work badly, slowly or not at all, everyone suffers.

## Reflecting (I'm OK – You're OK)

At the outset of their relationship, Edward treated Susan with respect. When he spoke to her he meant what he said and had no hidden agenda. Susan reflected back a light that was true and uncorrupted.

When we respect ourselves and we respect others, we are deeply connected to our Inner Warrior. The result is that we can confidently, honestly and unemotionally put our views, needs or wants on the table and also feel able to accord the same possibility to others.

### EQUILIBRIUM RESTORED

After our session, Susan attended another boardroom meeting during which she could see that once again Edward's colleagues were also getting frustrated by his being irrationally obstructive. Rather than use this to engender her usual attacking frame of mind, she instead chose to be a decent human being. Calmly and rationally she looked him in the eye, saw within him his Not-OK Lamb, rather than merely his Hijacker behaviour, and empathically asked him to expand on the point he was making.

Somewhat taken aback by the composed yet sympathetic manner she exhibited, Edward visibly relaxed and a professional dialogue ensued. This did not go unnoticed in the rest of the group; soon an engaged egoless working discussion was taking place. For the first time in a long time, the meeting was not about political games, but making real decisions and achieving results.

Her success in the boardroom setting impacted on her subsequent meetings with Edward on an individual basis. No longer was he someone to be feared; instead he was a colleague with whom she was able to work easily and therefore once more give of her best.

## IGNORING THE STUB MARKS

During my career I was a volunteer with Relate. One of my most difficult assignments was with a husband who had been physically abusing his wife for many years. During our first session, in order to explain the extent to which he had been abusive the husband asked his wife to lift up her sleeve. When she did so, I saw that the skin of her arm was covered with cigarette burns.

My initial internal reaction was one of distaste. If I had gone with this feeling I would have spoken to this man as if he were an absolute reprobate. He would probably then have either left the room or shouted back at me. Nothing would have been learnt and the abuse would have continued. Trained as I was, however, in the concepts above, I was able to see him as an *OK human being* even though I strongly disapproved of his *behaviour*. I calmly asked him to tell me more and was able to create a collaborative atmosphere in which he felt able to discuss his past behaviour openly and learn how he might change.

If we are serious about creating learning environments where people feel safe to say what is on their minds, we need to be able to feel OK about ourselves and others: no matter what they say or do, we can always have compassion for them as human beings. How to hold this philosophy in our *head* in order to *feel* this way is what we are going to cover in the next chapter.

# CHAPTER 10

# CONSENSUS

## CASE STUDY

Management meetings at a telecommunications company were populated by the following people: Keith Chandler, the operations director, who used silences and sarcastic retorts to intimidate and get his own way. He is frequently in conflict with Julian Burford, the quality manager, who is normally collaborative but will scrap with Keith if he needs to. Daniel Ward, the MD, would like to be a more effective leader – unfortunately he feels threatened by Keith and gets pleasure from seeing Julian stand up to him. Bob Jennings, the HR director, is placating and compassionate. June Walsh, the head of engineering, is usually silent but sometimes voices agreement with Keith, a fellow engineer. Mario DeCosta, the finance director, maintains as low a profile as possible.

## Microcosm Moment

The atmosphere between Keith and Julian is especially fraught as Julian is angered by Keith's refusal to let some of his people join a quality improvement team that Julian not only sees as vital if he is to meet his targets but also passionately believes will improve the organization.

Bob, as usual, is trying to calm things down by seeing both sides of the argument. In the meantime, both June and Keith occasionally steal furtive glances at each other – the glances of clandestine allies. Daniel comes in every now and again, ostensibly trying to diffuse the situation but secretly enjoying watching Julian stand up to Keith.

After a lot of pain for Julian and the rest of the team, Keith, having demolished Julian's enthusiasm, makes a show of giving in. (In reality, he couldn't have been less cooperatively minded if he had asked Julian to nail his feet to the floor and then gallop.) This leaves a sour taste in Julian's mouth – he's got what he wanted but at the expense of his well-being, self-respect and image in the eyes of the rest of the team. For, like everyone else, he knows there'll be no follow-through.

Management meetings in this company were something that everyone had come to dread. They were necessary and could not be avoided but the atmosphere was always cold and most team members felt isolated. Because of this, discussions were stilted, decisions were difficult to come by and commitment to agreed actions was rarely adhered to.

Daniel had asked me to come and work with him and his team because he was at a loss to know how to prevent meetings being dominated by Keith. After observing such a meeting, I demonstrated how a number of them were either avoiding, accommodating or compromising out of the anxiety created by the prospect of yet another abusive outburst by Keith.

The fact that everyone knew that Keith was not arguing for the good of the business only added to the fear culture. If he had been aggressive and domineering in defence of a legitimate business argument, this would have been a pill people maybe could have swallowed. However, those present were only too aware his real agenda was simply to impair Julian's enthusiasm regardless of the issue at stake.

Strong leadership could have acted as a break on Keith's behaviour. Unfortunately, Daniel was not prepared to confront him, even though he himself could be on the receiving end of Keith's sharp tongue. With no example to follow, most of the team felt impotent.

I emphasized that if they were ever to create an environment in which everyone felt safe to speak they would all, including Keith, have to carry out debates from the collaborative, I'm OK – You're OK, problem-solving box.

This led them to the predictable comment: Ah, that's all well and good but how do you do it? My response was to show them what they had been doing before my intervention. Then show them how to correct it.

## WHAT MAKES US ANXIOUS AT WORK?

Keith's aggressive behaviour in team meetings was creating unnecessary stress for other team members. I later found, on mentoring Keith, that his manner made many of his direct reports anxious, too.

Very few of us will enjoy the luxury of a workplace where there is nothing that makes us anxious. Most of us can name at least one source of concern to us. Here are some 'triggers' that clients have told me when asked what makes them anxious at work. When asked what triggers them not to stay in the collaborative box, the list includes:

- 'Constantly correcting other people's mistakes'
- 'Family arguments'
- 'My boss. He seems to have such a low opinion of me'
- 'An obstructive colleague'
- 'Long hours'
- 'My relatives at Christmas'
- 'Fear of redundancy'
- 'Awkward team meetings'
- 'Feeling powerless'
- 'Bullying'

## RESPONSE TO 'THREATS'

Why do people react to these situations with anxiety? Being animals, our bodies unconsciously mobilize energy in order to be ready to respond to threats in our environment. This mobilization occurs through the action of both the sympathetic nervous system and the endocrine system, such that noradrenaline, adrenaline and glucose are released into the blood system.

The effect on us is shallow breathing which occurs in order to oxygenate the blood which is being pumped quickly to muscles which have tensed (hence 'butterflies in the stomach'): ready for 'fight' or 'flight'. Our digestion slows down so that the blood is no longer pumped to the stomach, which in turn leads to a dry mouth. In the meantime we find our mind is racing or has gone completely blank.

This fight or flight response was necessary and useful when as cavemen we were confronted by a wild animal and had to decide whether to kill it for lunch or run for our lives! Wild animals, particularly hungry wild animals, have the potential to be a real threat to us.

We still have the same response today when we encounter a threat in our environment, but the ways in which we express fight and flight now are very different.

When Keith is being aggressive, he is feeling threatened by the possibility that Julian will excel and usurp his dominant position in the team. Accordingly he tends to express fight by being abusive, sarcastic and disparaging to Julian in meetings. Other ways we express fight may be hitting, shouting, slamming doors, standing nose-to-nose with another, pushing and shoving.

Most of the rest of the team react to threat using flight. Mario, for example, tries to opt out of the proceedings altogether, clamming up and withdrawing. Daniel yields to Keith's bid for the leadership. Other ways of expressing flight are removing ourselves from the situation, manipulation, withholding, avoiding, taking time off, seeking solace in alcohol or drugs, giving in or giving up.

Both of these can be expressed in terms of specific body language and non-verbal communication. For fight, these might include staring, going red in the face, appearing threatening, banging a fist on the table, throwing rather than putting down an object. For flight, they might include blushing, cringing, lack of eye contact, stuttering, covering your face, daydreaming and fidgeting.

Do either of these types of activity generally solve the problem? The answer is usually no, they either prolong it or exacerbate it.

## TRIGGERS ARE SOURCES NOT CAUSES OF TENSION

By viewing the situation as a threat our adrenalin will flow and we experience a surge of emotion – anger or anxiety – and respond accordingly. To be effective, what we need to do instead is stay in a calm, objective, problem-solving mode. How can we do that? The first stage is to not view problems as threats. Go back to the list of 'What makes you anxious at work?' and ask yourself if each is a threat or a problem to be solved:

- Is correcting other people's mistakes a threat or a problem to be solved?
- Are family arguments a threat or a problem to be solved?
- Is the boss who has a low opinion of you a threat or a problem to be solved?
- Is an obstructive colleague a threat or a problem to be solved?
- Are long hours a threat or a problem to be solved?
- Are your relatives at Christmas a threat or a problem to be solved?
- Is fear of redundancy a threat or a problem to be solved?
- Are awkward team meetings a threat or a problem to be solved?
- Is feeling powerless a threat or a problem to be solved?
- Is bullying a threat or a problem to be solved?

A key skill to being a Warrior is the ability to change the way we view any given situation – and no longer view problems as threats. If we want to react differently to those situations that caused us to get into fight or flight then we need to *view* them differently (see Figure 10.1).

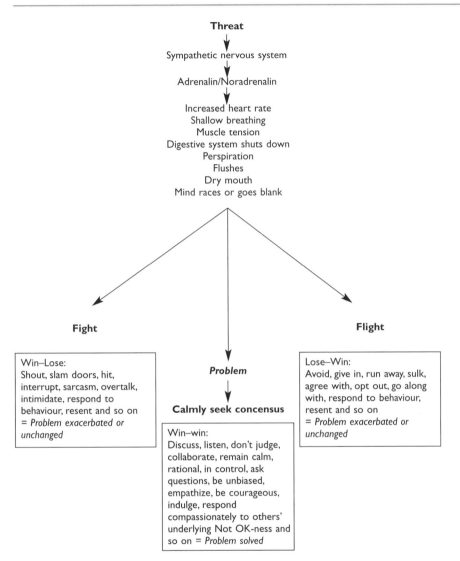

**Figure 10.1** Effects of viewing 'threats' as problems

## THOUGHTS CAUSE FEELINGS

Most of us imagine that the way we feel and, hence, our reactions depend entirely on the situation in which we find ourselves. We assume that we are not responsible for our reaction, but instead, the other person or situation is.

In other words, we are saying a situation alone dictates our feelings and subsequent behaviour:

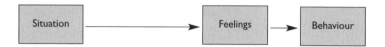

My client Stephen Miller would say to me about his boss, Graham Dawson, 'Graham should never have been given that job. He's controlling and is so detail oriented in his work it's enough to drive anyone nuts. Is it any wonder I slag him off?'

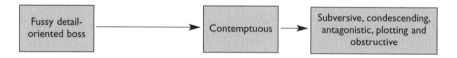

But although Stephen finds Graham's meticulous style results in his feeling contemptuous, another person might feel happy because Graham complements their own very different style. A third person may feel indifferent because they intend to leave the company and don't care either way. A fourth person might decide it's time they learnt to appreciate a diametrically opposed style to their own and relish the challenge.

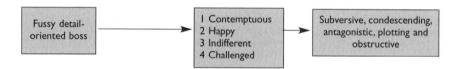

So we have four people, and four different feelings about the same situation.

It is clear, therefore, that a situation alone does not make us feel anything. The difference between all four is the way they view the situation: their perception, their interpretation, the way they *think* about it.

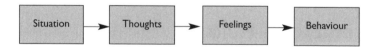

If we think negatively about ourselves or the other person we are likely to feel bad and respond with fight or flight. Stephen consistently expressed his negative thoughts about Graham:

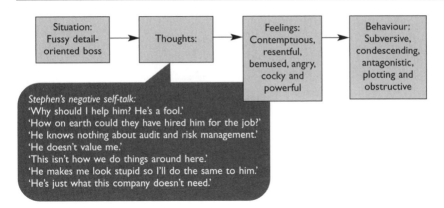

Sometimes Stephen felt good about himself and bad about Graham (I'm OK – You're Not OK) and behaved aggressively in team meetings. At other times, Stephen felt bad about himself and Graham (I'm Not OK – You're Not OK) in which case he resorted to passive–aggressive behaviour such as deliberately misunderstanding him.

## THINK POSITIVE, THINK CONSENSUS!

In order for Stephen to be able to develop a win–win, collaborative, I'm OK – You're OK, working relationship with Graham he had to learn to change his negative self-talk and replace it with positive thoughts:

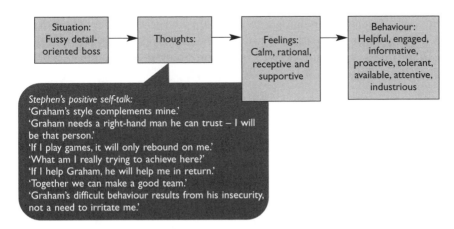

By changing his *thoughts* about his situation with Graham, Stephen changed the way he *felt* towards him, which in turn influenced the way he behaved for the better.

He learnt to see Graham's working style with new eyes and where he still had reservations he was able to raise them in a constructive non-confrontational way. He was able to stay in the right-hand, collaborative box and seek win–win consensus.

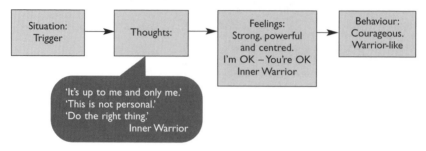

## DON'T TAKE IT PERSONALLY

The only thing that's stopping us feel OK in, or about, any given situation is our thoughts. We can influence the way we feel and behave by tuning into and changing the way we think – about ourselves, others, our situation and life.

The rules of engagement we develop as children, as we have seen, will have an impact on our behaviour as adults. These rules are often so well integrated that we are not conscious of their influence on us. By responding to a set rules from the past we prevent ourselves from being versatile in the present situation.

These rules are represented in our heads in the form of 'shoulds', 'oughts' and 'musts'. When we are up against what we perceive as a threat to our equilibrium, we may resort to self-talk that demands others to live by our rules. As Hijackers we will consciously or unconsciously be thinking such thoughts as:

- 'You should listen to me!'
- 'You ought to do it my way!'
- 'You must agree!'

When responding to a threat as a Lamb, our internalized rules will result in such unconscious or conscious thoughts as:

- 'I should be polite and pleasant.'
- 'I ought to put other people first.'
- 'I must not look foolish.'

And when behaving as a Shadow our thoughts will accuse both the other and ourselves of transgressing the rules.

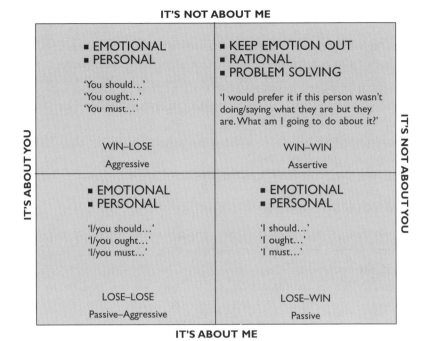

**IT'S NOT ABOUT ME**

| | |
|---|---|
| ▪ EMOTIONAL<br>▪ PERSONAL<br><br>'You should...'<br>'You ought...'<br>'You must...'<br><br><br>WIN–LOSE<br>Aggressive | ▪ KEEP EMOTION OUT<br>▪ RATIONAL<br>▪ PROBLEM SOLVING<br><br>'I would prefer it if this person wasn't doing/saying what they are but they are. What am I going to do about it?'<br><br>WIN–WIN<br>Assertive |
| ▪ EMOTIONAL<br>▪ PERSONAL<br><br>'I/you should...'<br>'I/you ought...'<br>'I/you must...'<br><br><br>LOSE–LOSE<br>Passive–Aggressive | ▪ EMOTIONAL<br>▪ PERSONAL<br><br>'I should...'<br>'I ought...'<br>'I must...'<br><br><br>LOSE–WIN<br>Passive |

IT'S ABOUT YOU (left) — IT'S NOT ABOUT YOU (right)

**IT'S ABOUT ME**

**Figure 10.2** Accessing your Inner Warrior

*Source:* Adapted from Thomas and Kilmann, 1974

When our internal 'shoulds', 'oughts' and 'musts' result in our viewing the circumstances as personal – about them or about us – our response is liable to be an unskilful attack either on the other person or on ourselves. If, for example someone throws a report we've written back at us and says 'I've never seen anything as bad as this!' a Hijacker may respond with 'You think that's bad, you should hear what I think of the one you gave me last week!'. In contrast, a Lamb may respond with 'I know. I'm dreadful at writing reports.'

If, instead, we choose to replace our shoulds, oughts and musts with a conscious sentence geared to the ongoing situation, we are likely to feel calmer and behave collaboratively. Saying to ourselves something like 'I would prefer it if this person were not overtaking me but they are, so what am I going to do about it?' instantly poses what was perceived as a threat now as a problem to be solved.

For Lambs and Shadows, this thought provides the basis for accessing our Inner Warrior and behaving with the power of a Warrior. For Hijackers, it encourages us to choose a more rational and compassionate response. This is illustrated in Figure 10.2.

## NO ONE CAN MAKE US FEEL ANYTHING

People find a multitude of different reasons why they cannot access their Inner Warrior and behave as a Warrior. Common justifications are:

- 'I've got a mortgage to pay and can't risk getting the sack'
- 'There will be a terrible atmosphere if I fall out with them. I can't work in that environment'
- 'I'll get the sack'
- 'My annual bonus will suffer'
- 'Why rock the boat? Nothing changes'
- 'They always win in the end'
- 'I don't want to upset them'

People who avoid, accommodate or compete will not achieve happiness and success in the long term. Nor will they contribute to the happiness and success of the company.

We cannot blame circumstances for the way we feel and behave. No

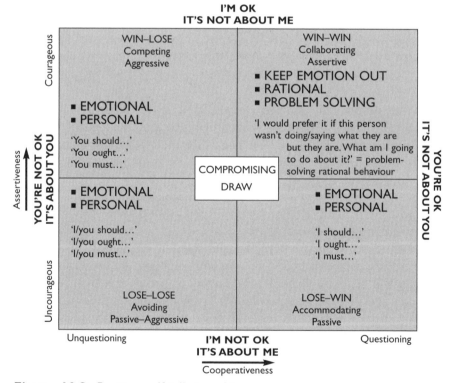

**Figure 10.3** Positive self-talk to achieve consensus

Source: Adapted from Thomas and Kilmann, 1974

one can make us feel anything. Not angry, not frightened, not stupid, not sad. If we fear someone in a meeting will 'make' us feel stupid, we have to remember that how we feel is in our hands, it will depend on how we interpret what has been said. If we decide to see it for what it is, an ego-defensive smokescreen to stop the other person looking stupid; a tactic to make us look stupid; a clumsy diversion or merely a lack of skill and *choose* to view it as of minimal significance to *our* ego, we can stay relaxed and confident and achieve a win–win consensus (see Figure 10.3).

Each individual in our teams has their own way of managing disagreement. At times, we see each other as a threat. Because of this the prevailing tendency of the group dynamic is for some team members to get into flight and some to get into fight. Apart from one or two intermittent appeals to reason, no one appears to show the required *compassion* for anyone else's present situation and this is often the main reason for the high degree of tension in the team.

# CHAPTER 11

# COMPASSION

## CASE STUDY

Adrian Norwich is a marketing manager at an aviation company who reported directly to Andrew Reed, the sales and marketing director, until a deputy director, Jeremy Harding, was brought in. He felt put out by the fact that he was one level below; this feeling was exacerbated by the fact that three others in his team continued to report to Andrew.

As a result he resented Jeremy, who was by nature a thorough, bureaucratic type who had for some time thrived in the political environment of his previous firm. Jeremy needed to cover his back and was cautious about ensuring that he did not give others the opportunity to criticize him for anything. Adrian, by contrast, had a tremendous sense of integrity, which he tended to express as an autonomous maverick.

Adrian's behaviour manifested itself in two ways. At times he used his Inner Warrior inappropriately by getting aggressive with Jeremy. For example, he would routinely lambaste his character and performance to other colleagues in corridor meetings. The second form of behaviour was passive–aggressive. During meetings Adrian would be obliquely rude about Jeremy's approach in his presence. This approach is demonstrated in my microcosm moment.

## Microcosm Moment

Adrian would deliberately misunderstand what Jeremy was saying. One day, Jeremy approached him in the office: 'Hi Ade. You know I've got that update meeting with the MD tomorrow? Just out of interest, have you heard anything about how Sales are feeling about the new campaign?' Adrian thought for a moment, smiled thinly, and replied, 'Sorry Jeremy, I haven't heard anything because I haven't asked anyone. Would you like me to ask?'

Jeremy shook his head vehemently. 'No, don't ask anyone. But what have you heard?'

Adrian knew full well that Jeremy just wanted to know what the rumours were so that he felt more confident before walking into the meeting the next day. But he would not help him. He replied once more that he had heard nothing because he had asked no one. He took the question literally, refusing to show compassion for Jeremy's obvious predicament.

## THE LITTLE TENT MODEL

This passive–aggressive, I'm Not OK – You're Not OK stance leaves both Jeremy and Adrian in a lose–lose position. Indeed, I was asked to work with Adrian after he had been given a written warning for his uncooperative manner.

I showed Adrian how his bad feelings about himself and Jeremy were the result of his taking the change in reporting lines personally (It's about me – It's about you). This was clearly ineffective. Handling conflict by either avoiding or competing may feel like a short-term win but in the long run he was losing. Far from solving his problem, his behaviour had resulted in the problem initially remaining the same until eventually it was exacerbated. Stacking up resentment and avoiding dealing with issues had blocked his ability to work well.

For Adrian to become the collaborative colleague he once was, he will need to change the way he feels about himself and his 'provoker' – Jeremy. This will require his changing the way he views the 'provocation' – Adrian's demotion caused by Jeremy's new position. If he can do this, he will be able to keep his job, return to his authentic self and be in the running for the promotion he craves.

This approach mirrors that of the 'big tent' philosophy, which is the belief that political groups should cast aside differences and make room for people with various and opposing views. The following Little Tent model summarizes how we can do this in our relationships using the previous four Cs. When someone begins a sentence or walks towards you, their tone or posture will make it obvious that you are about to be caught up in a confrontation. You will have a number of seconds to complete the following four steps:

1. *Note your physiological changes and relax:* Notice your instant stress reaction to the 'threat' – increased heart rate, blushing, muscle tension or whatever – and see it as a sign that you are likely to respond unskilfully with either fight or flight behaviours. Then take a deep breath and as you breath out say silently to yourself the word 'Relax' and then relax your muscles whilst thinking the words 'It's not about me and it's not about you – it's an interesting point of view' four times. With practice this sentence will urge you to follow to the next three stages:

2. *Change the way you view the provoker:* Think to yourself that he or she is OK as a human being, 'I just don't like what they're saying or doing right now. Most people are feeling Not OK no matter how they behave. I need to respond to this and feel compassionate towards them.'

3. *Change the way you view the provocation:* Whatever the issue at hand, it's not personal, it's just an interesting point of view. 'My heart rate doesn't have to go up one jot. Let's start at 50/50 – he or she may be 100% right or I may be. Alternatively the answer may lie somewhere in the middle. Let's discuss it and see.'

4. *Problem solve:* To show empathy, compassion and collaboration – ask a question. Say something like 'That's interesting, what makes you say that?' Don't make a statement as you'll either get into I'm OK – You're Not OK or I'm Not OK – You're OK. And remember, you don't have to win! This is not a subtle way of manipulating people.

## WHY COMPASSION?

Why show compassion? Because, by being compassionate we will treat others with integrity and, in so doing, help them to regain their integrity and feel good about themselves.

In languages that derive from Latin, 'compassion' means: we cannot look on coolly as others suffer; or, we sympathize with those who suffer. That is why the word 'compassion' generally inspires suspicion; it designates what is considered a second-rate sentiment that has little to do with love. To love someone out of compassion means not really to love them.

In languages such as Czech, Polish, German and Swedish, which form the word 'compassion' from the root 'feeling', the word is given a broader meaning: to have compassion (co-feeling) means not only to be able to live with others' misfortune but also to feel with them any emotion – joy, anxiety, happiness, pain.

This kind of compassion therefore signifies the maximal capacity of the art of emotional telepathy: empathy. Compassion can be a joy when used suitably but a curse when overused such that our goodwill is abused. Being a spiritual person does not mean being a doormat.

Whether we are overly compassionate or insufficiently so, the following technique will help us to:

- Clarify what we are doing in our relationships with others
- Appreciate the impact this has on ourselves and others
- Choose more effective methods of operating

Using a second aspect of transactional analysis, we can begin to analyse the sources and structure of our behaviours.

## OUR EGO STATES

We can observe quite distinct types of behaviour which seem to come from different sources within ourselves. These three *ego states* are called Parent, Adult and Child. None of these states has anything to do with a person's age. You can observe very young children exhibiting them when playing, say, 'mummies and daddies'.

# 1. The Parent

This state contains the attitudes, feelings and behaviour incorporated from external sources, primarily parents. In our outward behaviour it is expressed in two ways:

- *Nurturing Parent* – concerned with caring, loving and helping
- *Critical Parent* – criticizing, censuring and punishing

This is the part of us that may react to external demands or conflict by being autocratic.

## 2. The Adult

This state contains those behaviours concerned with collecting information, organizing and analysing. It operates dispassionately and without emotion.

In the Adult mode we often react to external demands or conflict by initiating: by having the courage to both assert our own opinion whilst equally being open to hear and understand that of others.

## 3. The Child

This state contains all the behaviours that come naturally to a child, but just as the Parent has different facets, so does the Child. The Child develops into three parts – the Free Child, the Adapted Child and the Little Professor.

■ *Free Child* – is spontaneous, energetic, curious, loving and uninhibited: the part of us that feels free and loves pleasure. We transact freely and openly with others. We respond with love and affection when our needs are met and angry rebellion when they are not. We see Free Child expressed at football matches when as grown ups we use rattles! We also see Free Child in the Hijacker, demanding they get their own way by continuing to metaphorically stamp their feet in meetings. Many of us, however, repress our Free Child and overstress our Parent instead.

■ *Adapted Child* – our Adapted Child developed when we learnt to change (adapt) our feelings and behaviour in response to the world around us. Learned feelings of guilt, fear, depression, anxiety, jealousy and pride are characteristic of the Adapted Child. It's through such adaptations we become socialized and learn, for example to share, to take turns and be friendly. We must learn these skills to get along socially – saying 'please', 'thank you' and 'I'm sorry'. It is the part of us that feels Not OK if we are:

– Frightened to speak before an audience
– Depressed when someone criticizes our work
– Hurt when things don't go our way at a meeting
– Anxious when important deadlines confront us

The adapted child can become the most troublesome part of ourselves. When in the Adapted Child we often react to external demands and conflict by being a Lamb or Shadow – complying, sulking or avoiding situations and results in our:

– Trying to please everyone

– Turning our back on people with problems
– Putting off work until a deadline passes

■ *Little Professor* – is the thinking part of our Child and is creative, intuitive and manipulative. The Little Professor can:
– Dream up new ideas
– Intuitively sense how to solve a problem

It is the part that knows how to get what we want by sensing when to cry, pout or shout. We use our Little Professor when we are being versatile. Our Little Professor helps us to work creatively with people such that we seek ways to understand their needs and cooperate with their achievement of them whilst simultaneously influencing them to do the same with our own.

## RECOGNIZING EGO STATES

Once you begin to identify your own ego states, it is easy to recognize the states of others. Table 11.1 may help you in this process.

It is possible not only to recognize our ego states, but also to develop the ability to switch them at will – moving from a Nurturing Parent to an analytical Adult, to a fun-loving Child without too much difficulty. Some of us find this easier than others. Often we have favourite ego states and tend to stick with those.

Some of us are always criticizing or helping others: the constant Parent. Some of us continually analyse and prefer facts to feelings: the constant Adult. Some of us operate with strong feelings all the time, consumed with anger, aggression or guilt – looking for kicks, or feeling helpless: the constant Child.

Interestingly, much of the behaviour I observe in organizations is of counterdependent adolescents who respond to authority by doing, or

| | | | Table 11.1 Recognizing ego states | | | |
|---|---|---|---|---|---|---|
| | **Critical Parent** | **Nurturing Parent** | **Adult** | **Free Child** | **Adapted Child** | **Little Professor** |
| **Words** | Should, ought, must, don't | Excellent, brilliant, well done, there there | How, why, who, what, when, yes, no | Fun, want, mine, need | Can't, wish, please, thank you, I can wait | I've got an idea, pl–e–a–s–e, now |

believing, the opposite of what they are told. They veer between Critical Parent and Child: the constant Adolescent.

## REFLEXIVE RESPONSES

A transaction is an exchange between two people. In our transactions, we each speak from one of our three ego states. To be successful, transactions must be complementary, if they are crossed then the conversation either changes its nature or ends – often abruptly.

## I. Complementary Transactions

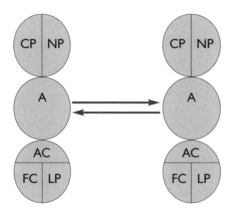

ADULT: 'Where is the report?'
ADULT: 'It's on your desk.'

## 2. Crossed Transactions

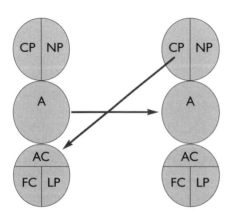

ADULT TO ADULT: 'Where is the Report?'
CRITICAL PARENT TO ADAPTED CHILD: 'Can't you find anything for yourself?'

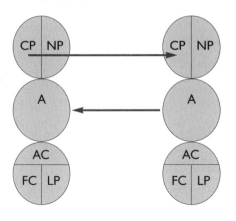

CRITICAL PARENT TO CRITICAL PARENT: 'Isn't Jennifer useless?'
ADULT TO ADULT: 'I don't have any experiences of her work.'

## Transactions Change over Time

Many romantic relationships turn sour after a year or two. When we first see someone across a crowded room our subconscious mind says to ourselves 'that person is everything I am not. They will make me whole.' And for several months, we love the fact that, whereas we would leave for a trip with a passport and toothbrush, they needed a plan, a map and a thermos. Eventually, however, these differences begin to irritate and we spend the rest of our lives trying to make them the same as ourselves.

So, whereas we communicated from Adult to Adult or Nurturing Parent to Child, now most conversations are of the kind above, from Critical Parent to Child.

*From the first few months of a relationship:*

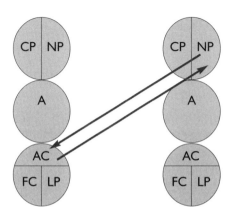

ADAPTED CHILD TO NURTURING PARENT: 'I have a headache.'
NURTURING PARENT TO ADAPTED CHILD: 'You sit down and I'll get you the painkillers and some tea.'

*To:*

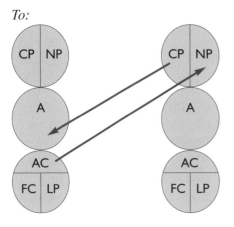

ADAPTED CHILD TO NURTURING PARENT: 'I have a headache.'
CRITICAL PARENT TO ADULT: 'You know where the painkillers are kept...'

A similar shift in our transactions occurs after the honeymoon period at the office. Simply being aware of this model, regaining our compassion and consciously being a Nurturing Parent to the Not OK child in others, can radically change an atmosphere that has built up between two people. We cannot change the way others behave, but by initially being the bigger person, responding to their child and refusing to be drawn, we can influence them to collaborate: Adult to Adult.

## 3. Duplex Transactions

Returning to Adrian, when he was deliberately misunderstanding Jeremy, he was participating in a duplex transaction:

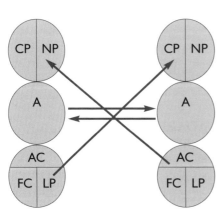

JEREMY – ADULT TO ADULT: 'Do you know what the sales team think?'
ADRIAN – ADULT TO ADULT: 'No, would you like me to ask them?'

*Underlying meaning*:

JEREMY – ADAPTED CHILD TO NURTURING PARENT: 'Help me look good in front of the MD.'
ADRIAN – LITTLE PROFESSOR TO CRITICAL PARENT: 'Me help you? You have got to be joking!'

Because he viewed Jeremy as a threat, Adrian tried to undermine his authority by resorting to childlike behaviour. He did so automatically, even though he was dissatisfied with his reactions. He had no doubt that he was right to fight for justice, but knew he was doing so in a way that lacked integrity.

He recognized that he was behaving like a Child – or Adolescent – either Hijacking meetings or becoming a Shadow of his former self. If he is to regain his self-respect and that of Jeremy, Adrian must tap back into his Little Professor and be creative about his response to his situation. He began to realize that his boss was seeking support – a right-hand man he could trust – and that this was an opportunity to help Jeremy be a success. By viewing the situation and Jeremy from a different perspective, a load lifted off his shoulders and the way forward was not only obvious but also one that suited his honest and compassionate nature.

## COMPASSION REQUIRES VERSATILITY

Skilled communicators are able to adjust their styles to suit their audience. Encouraging people to participate collaboratively will mean their becoming sensitive to their preferred styles and then using their Little Professor to respond more effectively. The following are suggestions of how to be compassionate and indulge 'the wisdom of the difference' with each of the four styles:

*With Lambs (ACs):*
- Identify the rationale
- Proceed caringly
- Support them emotionally
- Talk about their personal life
- Provide initiative and direction
- Be gentle, specific and harmonious

*With Hijackers (CPs):*
- Identify the objective
- Proceed rapidly
- Support their results
- Talk about immediate action
- Provide freedom and autonomy
- Be businesslike, time conscious and factual

*With Shadows (ACs):*
- Identify the method
- Proceed deliberately
- Support their principles
- Talk about documented facts
- Provide deadlines and follow-ups
- Be patient, organized and logical

*With Warriors (A):*
- Identify the personnel
- Proceed enthusiastically
- Support their vision
- Talk about people and ideas
- Provide discipline and focus
- Be stimulating, encouraging and flexible

## BE COMPASSIONATE AND INDULGE

Jeremy's approach to conflict is avoidance. In this respect he behaves as a Shadow. Adrian needs to consider the above list on how to show compassion and indulge the wisdom of the difference and, as an Adult, respond accordingly if he is to help Jeremy. Adults are rational problem solvers. In order to solve problems, we first need to obtain information. This means that in conversation we *ask questions*, seek clarification or summarize the discussion thus far. By doing this, others will experience our behaviour as reasonable, cooperative and empathic. When in our other ego states, we tend to *make statements* which, as we saw in Chapter 9, are not nearly as constructive. This is shown in Figure 11.1.

Once a question is asked, before responding to someone's point, paraphrasing what we think they mean can help both parties. It helps clarify whether what has been heard was what was meant: there may be confusion in the mind of the speaker, the listener or in the minds of both.

Beginning a response with the words 'Are you saying...?' can help check out the meaning before we go on to agree or disagree. Simply checking understanding will feel empathic, but is especially gratifying to the other person when we are correct in our understanding of what has been said.

Summarizing is equally collaborative, bringing together as it does all the contributions and restating them in a way that helps check if there is broad agreement about what has been said. Without frequent summaries,

| HIJACKER | Competitive/ Autocratic | Collaborative/ Problem solving | WARRIOR |
|---|---|---|---|
| CRITICAL PARENT/ ADOLESCENT | | | ADULT |
| **MAKE STATEMENTS TO DEFEND OR ATTACK** | | **ASK QUESTIONS** | |
| I'm not prepared to change my position... I must make my position quite clear... My view is clearly the most rational... I'm sure mine is the best way... If you don't do this I'll... I know best, you'd better... Do as you're told... | | Can we investigate the problem? What do we disagree about? My position is ... what's yours? What is mutually acceptable? Is there common ground between us? Where do we differ? How can we solve this? | |
| **SHADOW** | Avoiding/ Sulking | Accommodating/ Complying | **LAMB** |
| CHILD/ADOLESCENT | | | CHILD |
| **MAKE STATEMENTS TO AVOID** | | **MAKE STATEMENTS TO DEFEND OR COMPLY** | |
| I can't take responsibility for this decision... I'd prefer not to discuss that now... That is outside my brief... I won't be drawn on that... I have no comment on that... I'm not in a position to discuss... I don't see your point... | | I concede that point... I agree with you there... I'm prepared to accept that... I will do as you say... I don't want to offend you... You have convinced me... I'm glad we agree on this... | |

**Figure 11.1** Compassion in conflict – ask a question

discussions can wander aimlessly rather than focusing on what has been accomplished.

Once we have the courage to be ourselves, we need not only to make our own points but also to show a willingness to listen and understand those of others. Asking questions, paraphrasing and summarizing, rather than blocking with personal statements or oblique comments, requires us to be empathic, indulgent and compassionate. If we want to retain our integrity whilst helping others to do so too, we need to remain in our Adult, I'm OK – You're OK, collaborative state and begin with a question as illustrated in Figure 11.2.

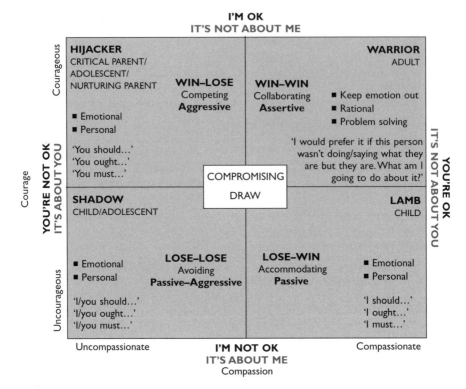

**Figure 11.2** Compassion in conflict

*Source:* Adapted from Thomas and Kilmann, 1974

# CHAPTER 12

# COURAGE

## CASE STUDY

Jon Bentley is 32 and a perfectionist who needs a structured timetable and the achievement of measurable targets to feel a success. However, his current project requires him to work with unreliable outsourced suppliers who agree to do one thing and then do another, missing targets and failing to achieve.

He has tried every way he can to leverage his suppliers to do the job they promise but has got nowhere. It's as if someone has pulled the rug from under him: the lack of control over his image in his own eyes and in that of others, along with the uncertainty he has over his daily output has become too much. He feels powerless and lost.

Jon has spent his life living in a logical, controlled environment. As soon as he was placed in one of ambiguity, without the rules and procedures he lives by, his only way out was to do more of the same. He simply worked harder, longer hours and made more and more timetables. This led to stress and exhaustion, but did not change his situation.

## Microcosm Moment

Jon is in the weekly update meeting with Gregory, his opposite number from the outsourced suppliers. He is trying to control his frustration. Gregory, once again, is giving umpteen reasons why he has not done what he said he would do. Jon cannot believe his ears. Gregory is contradicting himself by at one moment saying he did not recall the week's plan as Jon does and the next moment citing reasons why he was unable to implement it. His air of confidence cannot conceal his scorn for Jon and his position. Gregory is making obviously feeble excuses simply to fill the time before the meeting ends. Then he can get back to his personal agenda of keeping his own managers happy. On this occasion, Jon is attempting to appeal to Gregory's sense of fair play but since Gregory does not possess one, his words fall on deaf ears. Gregory makes the right noises but clearly has no intention of collaborating. As a result, Jon fears another week of failing to achieve his project plan. Yet as before, he cannot find a way to influence his suppliers to work to his plans.

His negative feelings about his suppliers and the lack of support from his boss, and his berating himself about his own inadequacy led to feelings of helplessness and hopelessness which resulted in depression. He now feels as if he's in a black hole. He has no sense of direction, no sense of himself; no light at the end of the tunnel.

## SUCCUMBING TO CATASTROPHIC FANTASIES

Jon is an extreme version of what can happen when we fear sticking our heads above the parapet and making a stand. Many of us, both leaders and followers, put up with behaviour that undermines our authority, our self-respect and our ability to successfully do our job. We avoid confronting aggressive or passive–aggressive individuals for fear of our 'catastrophic fantasies' coming to fruition. As I said in Chapter 1, catastrophic fantasies are catastrophic because we always think the worst and fantasies because they rarely happen. In Jon's case, his catastrophic fantasy was that if he was too confrontational with his suppliers they would sabotage his good name. The paradox is that by not taking the risk of confronting them, they sabotaged his good name.

Such fear of taking the risk of action can be the same for leaders as for followers. I am currently working with a director, Nilo, and his two deputies, Anneke and Kas, who have been leading their directorate without consistent follow-through. This allows Louis and Jeanne-Pierre – two of their team – to say one thing and then do another. This passive–aggressive stance permeates relationships throughout the directorate, leaving colleagues, clients and suppliers fighting a losing battle.

Nilo, Anneke and Kas avoid, accommodate or compromise their direct reports rather than endure a confrontation. They believe that living with obstructionism, procrastination, stubbornness and inefficiency is easier than experiencing the catastrophe they fantasize will occur if they conscientiously follow up on their directives. It is true that their strategy means they avoid the discomfort of handling conflict. However, they suffer instead the frustration of finding themselves wrong-footed in meetings with clients, the

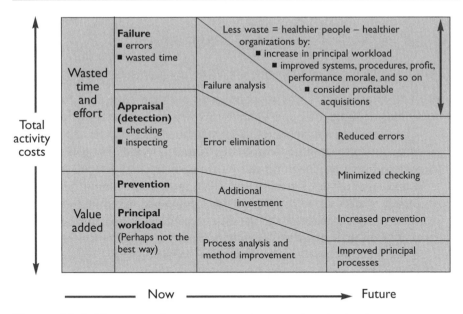

**Figure 12.1** The cost of wasting time due to others' mistakes

Board or their suppliers. It also allows the two passive–aggressive Shadows to demoralize the collaborative members of their team.

The result is that they spend more time *finding and correcting other people's failures*, than on their *principal* work. We decided that *preventing the failures* occurring in the first place by courageously confronting the game-players would save time, effort and 'face' in the future. This is illustrated in Figure 12.1.

When Nilo, Kas and Anneke courageously confronted Tony and Jeanne-Pierre, they were astonished to find not only did nothing awful occur but also both of them eventually ran out of excuses and learnt to fall in line with those doing an outstanding job. This improved morale for everyone in the directorate.

It might be worth counting how much time you have spent today uncovering, correcting or following up slip-ups made by others.

## CRUNCH MOMENTS

Once we realize that it is healthier for ourselves and our organization to speak up and say what is on our minds, we may still find it difficult to access the courage to do so when it comes to the crunch. We all face crunch moments. They pass quickly. It's now or never. It's fight or flight in preserving our values and those of the organization.

When you boil down life, when you look back on it, you can almost lay them out in a row. The following are a few key moments that I recall:

- A few years ago, I was shopping with my then 24-year-old daughter, Zelda, in Kingston-upon-Thames. We were about to walk into M&S when I noticed a distressed toddler standing in the middle of the pedestrian square crying uncontrollably. About 20 yards away his parents were looking on, laughing and mocking their child. I stood frozen, as did other shoppers, but implored Zelda to 'Do something!' She immediately walked up to the toddler, bent down and asked in a loud voice 'Are you lost, darling?' the parents stopped laughing came across and picked up their child whilst embarrassingly explaining to Zelda – and everyone watching – who they were. What courage, what speed of thought! A crunch moment I was unable to rise to.

- I was swimming in the Maldives with a friend when both of us were convinced that we saw a woman go under the water several yards ahead of us, and not resurface. I am not a strong swimmer but immediately swam towards the spot whereas my friend, Jonathan, swam back to shore. In fact, we were both mistaken and I could find no one in the water. When I asked him why he had done what he did, he shame-facedly explained he was going for help!

- My friend told me the following story. 'I remember I was nervous because we were passing through an Arab country and as a Jew I felt uneasy about this. We were standing in a queue in passport control when I heard a voice interrupt my thoughts behind me. A British Asian woman and her son were standing behind us. She was saying that she was nervous because she did not have a passport for her son, as was the case in those days. Much to the surprise of the person I was with, I instinctively waved her in front of us and said, "If they give you any trouble, I'll tell them we don't have children on passports in the UK." Sure enough, the two officials queried the lack of a passport for her son at which point I intervened as I had promised. The officials looked at my demeanour and, unquestioning, chose to take me at my word. The woman and her son were waved through.

  It was over 10 years ago and yet I can still clearly recall the sense of power I felt encircling me. Earlier I had had my own silly fantasies about what Arabs might do to a Jew passing through their country. Yet when I needed to take a lead I went into overdrive and became a leader.'

Everyone is a leader many times in their day-to-day lives. Whether we are followers – in that the formal hierarchy dictates that you are subordinate to others – or not, we all have leadership moments. Silly things like being the only one to stand up and give our seat to a pregnant woman. Everyone sits silently planning to do it, but we are the one to stand up. We show that we live by our values which are stronger than succumbing to the catastrophic fantasy of looking foolish in a crowd. It is highly desirable that the application of leadership skills permeates the organization so that each and every organizational member acquires the capacity to become a leader in his or her own right.

## WHAT DO ALL THESE CRUNCH MOMENTS HAVE IN COMMON?

Crunch moments have in common the opportunity to live our values and be the person we are meant to be. To do so at will when each opportunity arises, we need to be conscious of a philosophy that furnishes us with the courage to act now – as Nike puts it, 'Just do it!' The following model is useful in this respect.

Going back to our case study, Jon was *doing* something he was not happy about – accommodating uncooperative suppliers. He spent a great deal of his time at work, lunch, driving home, during the evening *reflecting* on his situation – his sense of powerlessness. He took time *planning* to do things differently – confront the suppliers and demand compliance. And had he had the courage, he would have taken the risk of *experimenting* with his plan. This is a model of how we solve problems, learn and develop and is illustrated in Figure 12.2.

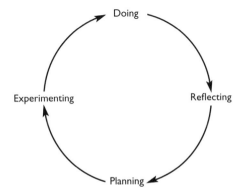

**Figure 12.2** How we learn to change

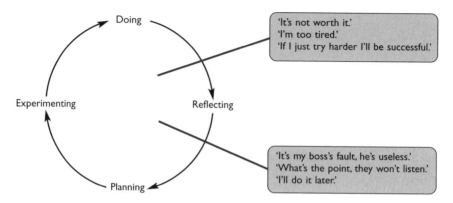

**Figure 12.3** How we sabotage our own change

But we can block ourselves from becoming everything we could be at each stage. Jon may have prevented himself from reflecting on his unhelpful behaviour of avoiding, accommodating or compromising, by saying to himself, 'It's not worth it', 'I'm too tired', 'If I just try harder I'll be successful'.

Even if Jon did take time to reflect on his situation, he may have prevented himself from planning to be courageous and authentic by such negative thinking as, 'What's the point, they won't listen', 'It's my boss's fault, he's useless' and 'I'll do it later'.

This is how we defend our ego. Instead of seeing our own behaviour as the source of discomfort and improvement, we use ego-defence mechanisms which keep us standing still in life. These defence mechanism include *blaming* ('It's my boss's fault'), *denial* ('It not that bad'), *rationalization* ('IT projects always stall'), *avoidance* ('I'm too busy to stop and think about it now') and so on.

Even when clients realize that accommodating, avoiding and compromising are harmful to themselves and the organization, they still find it difficult to speak up or take action when it comes to the crunch. The truth is that most of us spend much of our life going around the triangle in Figure 12.4. We spend a substantial amount of our time reflecting on our behaviour, situation or life; we make ambitious plans to change, yet when it comes down to it we do nothing.

- We think about asking for promotion, plan to do it, but don't
- We think about leaving our partner, plan to do it, but don't
- We think about starting a new life abroad, plan to do it, but don't
- We think about starting our own business, plan to do it, but don't
- We think about writing the book, plan to do it, but don't

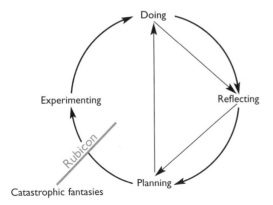

**Figure 12.4** Avoiding crossing Rubicons

- We think about doing something more meaningful with our life, plan to do it, but don't
- We think about confronting an obstructive colleague, plan to do it, but don't.

We do not act on our convictions. We do not cross the Rubicon. We avoid crossing Rubicons because of our catastrophic fantasies. Our 'top dog' is overridden by our underdog (Perls, 1971).

- Top dog is the part of us that tells us we are talented, unique and special. It promotes the belief that we can do anything we choose with our life and that we will surely be a success – the sky's the limit.
- Underdog then kicks in with a small yet unrelenting voice which warns us of what might go wrong, how much better others are and the advantages of remaining put.

As a result of the catastrophic fantasies of our underdog, we can spend weeks, months, even years going around the triangle. Reflecting on and planning to take a sabbatical and go travelling, to volunteer our services abroad, to make a name for ourselves; but we never do it. We never cross the Rubicon.

When it comes to the crunch, the thought of asking for a rise or promotion, starting the business, leaving the spouse, selling up and buying abroad or facing conflict feels risky. What stops us crossing Rubicons is fear of:

- The unknown
- Ambiguity
- Uncertainty

We fear uncertainty because we do not know whether or not we will:

- Win or lose
- Look clever or foolish
- Be a hero or a villain
- Be praised or punished
- Be popular or isolated
- Be better or worse off
- Succeed or fail

Crossing the Rubicon and speaking up for what we believe in can most certainly result in our feeling anxious. But how does it feel not speaking up, not being ourselves, not being recognized for who we are? How does life feel right now not taking the risks, keeping our heads down and being overlooked?

Either choice – remaining inauthentic or being authentic – is risky and provokes anxiety. But remaining inauthentic results in living a life of regret whilst being authentic offers the chance of living a life we can look back on with pride and satisfaction. We know life is one hundred per cent unpleasant right now but if we take a risk we have a fifty–fifty chance of it being better or worse. We can choose either:

- to keep our heads below the parapet and play it safe, knowing we are not living our one life to the full by contributing what we are capable of. We already regret lost opportunities – crunch moments – and look back saying 'If only I had...' Suffering the guilt of living an inauthentic, unfulfilled life is and will always remain, stressful, or
- to continually experiment with being ourselves and fulfilling our potential. This means living with the anxiety associated with the risks of uncertainty of jumping into the abyss, but it also brings the rewards of knowing you are 'doing it now!'

Life is inevitably stressful, but we make it worse for ourselves. We avoid crossing the Rubicon because of catastrophic fantasies. We imagine something awful will happen. Most of our catastrophic fantasies, however, are rarely catastrophic and nearly always fantasies. If we take the risks, we don't get the sack, people don't think badly of us, we are loved, we are successful.

There is no choice in life but to experience either the guilt of being like a Lamb led to the slaughter (or a Shadow of our former self) or the anxiety of being a Warrior and fulfilling our life's potential. Both are stressful but if we don't want to waste our life, in effect there is no choice.

One method of retaining the confidence to be a Warrior is to be realistic about the possible gains of taking risks as well as the possible losses. And one way to stop being a Lamb or a Shadow is to be realistic about the possible losses of not taking risks as well as the possible gains.

The fact is that confronting those who could sabotage our career is very risky. This is the catastrophic fantasy we all carry with us and could be real. Being authentic can be dangerous but the model of 'crossing Rubicons' reminds us that so too can living a meaningless, unfulfilled life.

As Rabbi Susya (1965) on his deathbed put it:

> When I get to Heaven they will not ask me 'Why were you not Moses? Instead they will ask 'Why were you not Susie? Why did you not become what only you could have become?

## WE NEED GOD TO PLAY A TRICK ON US

Before we cross Rubicons we need to clarify who we are, what we value and what we will fight for in life. An effective method is to imagine that God (or your Higher Power, Spirit or your own soul and so on) has said that you have ten more years to live and then he wants you back. The question asked is: What are you going to do with your ten years? And before you tell him (or her) you are going to 'travel', he adds that he wants you to spend the time making a significant contribution to the world!

Now it's ten years on and you are both looking down on people talking about you warmly on the day of your funeral. What are they saying? What do they remember about you? What do you want to be known for? Are they saying such things as:

- 'As an MP he made an amazing impact on rights for battered women.'
- 'As a member of the UN she was a forerunner in securing peaceful resolution to conflict.'
- 'His art brought joy to so many people.'
- 'As a TV journalist she contributed so much to ecology.'
- 'What an amazing family man/woman.'

Once you've hit on what you want to be known for, if God then said he (or she) was joking; that in fact you can do what you chose for the next 40 years, does it still feel right? If it doesn't, then choose again.

To paraphrase George Bernard Shaw, 'When you are lying on your deathbed looking back on your life it's not the things that you did that you'll regret, it's the things you didn't do.' You won't be lying and cringing about how you spoke up in a meeting in 2004, but asking yourself why didn't I ask for promotion, why didn't I start my own business, why didn't I confront the passive–aggressive Shadow or the aggressive Hijacker, why didn't I move to Florida, why didn't I fight for what I believed in? In the whole scheme of things are the little things that stress you now really so difficult to confront and overcome?

Looking back on our deathbed at 84, the idea of asking the person in another department to stop being obstructive will seem a trivial Rubicon to cross. By not taking the risk we are responsible for not being everything we could have been and could be.

Many people change their values and attitudes after a personal bereavement, spell in prison or financial downfall. What we want is for this to happen without a catastrophe. We need God to play us a trick. We don't want the share price to halve, we don't want a botched redundancy scheme communicated by text message. We want to avoid that.

When Jon understood the impact of not crossing his Rubicon on his health and that of the company, he found the courage to stand up for what he believed in. His action created a healthy group dynamic in his project team. Had he not taken action, he would be responsible for maintaining the unhealthy status quo.

As Irving Yalom (1980) puts it:

> One is entirely responsible for one's life, not only for one's actions but for one's failures to act.

## LIFE IS NOT ABOUT GETTING WHAT YOU WANT, IT'S ABOUT MEETING THE CHALLENGES ON THE WAY

The ideal existence is to be continually going around the cycle in an upward spiral; always learning, always changing, since there is no end to development.

For example, we may decide we want to experiment with handling conflict more effectively in our team meetings. We raise the idea in the Monday morning regular meeting and everyone agrees it's a great idea. So, when the opportunity arises, rather than sit in silence, today we tentatively express our feelings. All goes well for a short time until the momentum is lost with the usual suspects hijacking the conversation. Leaving the meeting, we reflect on our attempt to break out of our usual mode of operating, we learn from the experiment and plan how we will stay in the conversation next time. We experiment with this plan during the following meeting and find that our courage is rewarded by a decision that embraces our idea. And so we continue to develop the courage to live in

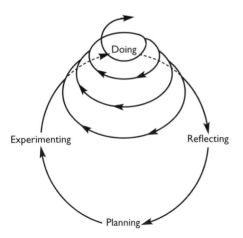

**Figure 12.5** The upward spiral of continuous improvement

harmony with our convictions. This spiral of continuous improvement is illustrated in Figure 12.5.

Sadly, many people come into the organization intending to develop themselves and the business but soon learn not to make waves. We may know a few colleagues who have had 10 years' experience but we also know those who have had one year's experience for 10 years.

Change programmes need to focus on awakening the Inner Warrior in each individual. We need to recognize that we are responsible for our own situation in life and for our desire to run away from our responsibility for it. For those of us who feel that others are unfair, unjust and diminishing our lives, it is important to remember that life is not about getting what we want, it is about meeting the challenges on the way. We must have the courage to cross our Rubicons every single day in the most heroic and compassionate way possible. Then our organizations can benefit from our talent and recognize our potential. This can only be good for ourselves and for the organization.

# CHAPTER 13

# EMBEDDING COURAGE AWARENESS

So where does all this leave us? Agreeably, it leaves us ready to implement everything we have learnt. We have a choice of interventions for our organization: I will explain how each one can be used in such a way as to enable our people to access their Inner Warrior and break the threads of the Gulliver Effect.

We have already seen that there are four outer persona present in every organization: the Warrior, the Lamb, the Hijacker and the Shadow. We have also seen that Hijackers and Habitual Shadows call the shots in many of these, resulting in an excess of Lamb and Shadow behavioural characteristics.

Our objective therefore is to help those who are straightjacketed in a single persona to find their *versatile self*. For in creating an individual who is *fully* connected to their Inner Warrior we bring about the ability to select at any given moment the appropriate persona for the situation. Remember, necessary skills are more than simply role competencies. The interpersonal skills of a Warrior can ultimately determine the difference between a functioning organization and one that excels. Connection to the Inner Warrior ensures they are evident.

If we are serious about harnessing the potential of all our people, acquisition of the Six Cs is essential. Collectively these bring: an understanding of the alienating capacity of conflict on ourselves; a checklist of dysfunctional behaviours in groups; the ability to facilitate a collaborative environment; the capability to remain calm, rational and in control; an understanding of the value of compassion; the ability to access courage so as to act immediately.

Sadly it is all too easy for the negative behaviour of one person to reverberate well beyond their immediate sphere of activity. Consider the following case study.

## CASE STUDY: 'I was just about to call you, Madam!'

Recently, I experienced first hand the corrosive effect of a habitual Shadow on the culture of an organization. This time it was as a customer. When my washing machine broke down, I called the manufacturer to order a replacement drum. I spoke to a manager at one of the depots, who asked which model I was using. In replying I read out the specification from a label on the machine. He informed me the drum would have to be ordered which would take two days. Then it would be delivered and fitted by an engineer.

When the engineer arrived it quickly became apparent that he'd brought the wrong drum. He remarked that this was a common occurrence, then returned to inform the depot manager. Somewhat put out, I telephoned the manager myself. When I spoke to him, he placed the blame for the mix-up squarely on my shoulders – suggesting I must have misread the label. However, I knew very well I had not and refused to accept responsibility. But though he then said he would arrange for the correct drum to be despatched, his barely concealed hostility told me this was going to be a bumpy ride.

The first indication of this was when I was informed that it would be a week – not two days – before the new part could be delivered. On the day it was due to be delivered I was still waiting at 1pm, five hours after the time agreed. I rang the manager to ask the reason for the delay and he informed me it was still being transported down from Birmingham. I then asked him when he was planning to tell me what was happening and he replied: 'I was just about to call you, Madam'. Three phone calls later (each time, having been told 'I was just about to call you, Madam'), the drum finally arrived at half past four. The two young engineers were clearly nervous as to my reaction, but I soon allayed their fears. I did not blame them for the chronically bad attitude of the depot manager. Once they realized this, they relaxed and opened up about their colleague. They told me that episodes such as this happened frequently. They confirmed my suspicions about his being a habitual Shadow, by revealing that he had only ordered the drum the previous day – therefore spitefully making me wait an extra week.

They appealed to me to make an official complaint, as they do with every customer in this predicament. In this way, I would be helping to undermine his position and hopefully contribute to getting him fired. When I asked if I could use their names in the complaint, they answered, 'Yes, we're the ones who have to deal with him every day.'

What a waste of decent human beings. And what a perfect example of how one passive–aggressive 'little Hitler' – if allowed free rein – is disproportionately powerful. He intimidates employees, he destroys customer good-will and is also costly due to the 'mopping up' needed after his 'mistakes'.

How do we remedy a culture that allows this situation to fester? There are several approaches I recommend:

## 1. THE NEW LEADERSHIP

We need leaders with antennae. Such leaders would have the capacity to see clearly the threads that bind certain members of their team; to sense a situation that undermines good people and that wastes their talent. A situation that some cannot tolerate. Why don't the leaders of the organization in the above case study sense the intimidatory nature of the depot manager? Because the problem remains veiled. They are not familiar with the concept of the four personas; nor with the Gulliver Effect; nor the significance of courage in personal and organizational development.

Leadership development therefore must focus on demonstrating the extent to which the Gulliver Effect influences executive team behaviours. They need to:

- *Sense the situation*: distinguish between Lambs, Shadows, Hijackers and Warriors
- *Know themselves*: their preferred style of operating and their choices
- *Know others*: recognize the behaviours in the team
- *Have the courage to eradicate the Gulliver Effect*: create a senior executive team climate that rewards courage and shows zero tolerance for the pursuit of personal agendas

Leaders must also develop the ability to see it at work in their own direct reports and in turn how it cascades down through each of their teams. Once they understand it, they can anticipate it and move to prevent it. They will:

- Recognize the human relations issues
- Raise them courageously
- Attack them skilfully
- Remedy them collaboratively and
- Remain vigilant in embedding values that are lived – not laminated

## 2. CULTIVATING WARRIORS

If we are serious about culture change we must start with the good people. We must get them to realize that it is their own fear of conflict that makes them allow themselves to be trodden on at work and elsewhere. Once they recognize the Gulliver Effect is a reality in their team and see their own part in it, we can begin a tailored training and development programme.

Such a programme will be designed to use the talent and potential of every member of the organization by encouraging individuals to exercise their courage in two critical ways:

- *Promote healthy debate:* We need people to promote healthy debate where blockages – whether interfunctional, interpersonal or related to business issues – are raised and dealt with as and when they arise.
- *Exhibit personal courage:* We need everyone to establish a personal value around their having the courage of their convictions. When they have a great idea, a concern or a disagreement they need to rise to their crunch moment and jump into the abyss. If we are to have our good people contribute fully to the organization, they must learn how to take the leap and land gracefully.

This will enable them to give of their best. It will also show them that their attitudes and behaviours are valued by the organization. Show them too that the organization wants to strengthen their influence over the culture and diminish that of the 'depot managers' of this world.

## 3. OD INDIVIDUAL-STYLE

It is eminently desirable that an organization has a vision, mission and set of value and objectives. But, be honest, how far does yours travel in truly achieving them in the spirit intended? For many organizations, bridging the gap between the stated and the real remains frustratingly difficult. Now consider for a moment if the very bedrock of our organization was formed of *courage*. We have already seen how important courage is in getting people to achieve their potential. To make a real difference, it is vital to design an OD intervention so that people know that acting with the courage of their convictions is encouraged and expected.

Without a doubt such an intervention would have made it easier for the washing machine engineers to act in accordance with their company's proclaimed values. They would have felt able to challenge their colleague's dysfunctional behaviour. The same applies to all the situations in the case studies. If Andy (see Case study, Chapter 7) had been working in an organization where courage underpinned the stated aims and values, he would have been able to confront a fault-line in his team instead of cloaking himself in anonymity for fear of provoking conflict.

If Susan (see Case study, Chapter 9) had worked in a courageous organization she would not have become institutionalized and as a result tongue-tied at crunch moments. Nor would she have hesitated to challenge Edward's bids for power and control. The truth is that whenever and wherever such people operate, their activities *can* be checked.

My recommendation is for your OD intervention to instil a common language, vision and groundswell around courage. Begin to view courage as a competency and benchmark it accordingly. Develop a culture and appraisal system that recognizes and rewards its use and application.

## THE ETHICAL IMPERATIVE

Today any progressive organization will strive to embrace the notion of participation and collaboration. Why do we want these things? Because we need them. Half a century's worth of formal research – not to mention thousands of years of experience – have shown that participative management leads to higher performance, greater productivity and more employee satisfaction. High participation levels are related to increased feelings of responsibility, better work relations, more positive attitudes towards work, and higher output (French and Caplan, 1973).

To change the perspective – we can also see that there are important ethical considerations at stake here too. Other research is telling us that when the three basic work-related needs of power, achievement and affection are not met, the result is physical (and psychological) damage to workers (Lassey and Sashkin, 1983). Consider the results from several studies that directly examined the effects of worker non-participation. Margolis, Kroes and Quinn (1974) found non-participation correlated with depression, escapist drinking and overall poor physical health – findings confirmed in other research studies.

On the basis of the above findings we make a compelling ethics-based case for compassionate leadership. In fact, a failure to demonstrate it is morally reprehensible. And needless to say it *will* adversely affect the bottom line.

## NO GAP TO MIND

Once you put this book down it will be time to act. Remember, whether your focus is with leadership, personal or organization development, you have to first recognize the Gulliver Effect, then confront it by training people in the Six Cs. If you implement the teachings contained in this book you will find there is no gap between theory and practice, between meeting culture and coffee machine culture, and between laminated values and those that are lived.

## The Gulliver Effect

- Conventional wisdom has it that people are resistant to change
- But people do change and usually for the worse
- They lose a sense of themselves
- They lack the courage of their convictions
- They waste their potential

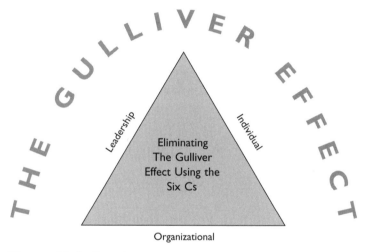

**Figure 13.1** Developing courage for personal and organizational change

## The Six Cs

*Conflict*

- We neglect to assert ourselves for fear of conflict means
- We instead accommodate, avoid and compromise
- This results in our resenting others but also ourselves
- A gap emerges between corridor meetings and real meetings
- The result is a lack of commitment to decisions

- Hence decisions are implemented idiosyncratically, slowly, badly or not at all
- Within leadership this means a lack of 'cabinet responsibility', leading to a silo-mentality
- Healthy organizations require that people are versatile and courageous enough to behave collaboratively when appropriate

## Concepts

- Accept that process issues are often of more significance than task issues
- Understand group dynamics so as to recognize what takes place in groups
- Identify who are the Hijackers, Lambs, Shadows and Warriors
- Use company values as a contract (or ground rules) for raising and developing interpersonal and group behaviour

## Collaboration

- Having the courage to remain collaborative in conflict means feeling good about ourselves and others
- Feeling bad about yourself or lacking confidence in relation to others will result in avoiding, accommodating or compromising
- Feeling negative or angry about others will result in attacking and over-competitive behaviour
- Feeling good about ourselves and others means that we can remain collaborative
- Remember that though we may not like what others are saying or doing, as a human being they're OK

## Consensus

- Since our *thoughts* influence our feelings we must be aware of and control our thoughts
- Thinking a 'threat' exists leads to flight (avoiding, accommodating and compromising) or fight (attacking, belittling and competing) behaviours
- Distinguish between real and imagined threats: most are merely problems to be solved
- So view them as a problems to be solved not as battles to be won
- Assume nothing and don't take things personally
- Begin by clarifying the other's position: ask a question

## Compassion

- Appreciate the wisdom of the difference between people
- Take the blinkers off and accept that your way is not the only way
- Experiment with different points of view and new ideas
- Be the bigger person and indulge accordingly
- You don't always have to win!

## Courage

- Remind yourself how stressful it is not being you
- Imagine how great life would be if you were being everything you knew you could be, recognized as the person you know you are and making your mark on life
- Crossing just one Rubicon will lead to an upward spiral
- Not crossing Rubicons leads only down
- There is really no choice in life but to have courage and take the risk of doing the right thing by yourself, others and the business

## HEROIC DIGNITY

There are times in our life when each of us has stepped into the abyss and flown rather than fallen. We know very well when we did – because we felt powerful, elated, alive. So we can do it. And there is nothing stopping us doing it more often, even all the time. Only ourselves.

Just imagine what going into work would feel like if we could be confident that we, along with all our colleagues, were heroic enough to be honest and have the courage of our convictions. That we all put as much effort into preserving our dignity as that of everyone else in the business.

We would no longer waste energy on dysfunctional group behaviours. Instead, we could use our time and effort tapping the creative potential of everyone in the organization to resolve business problems and collaboratively work towards agreed goals and objectives. Healthy people; healthy organizations.

My message is ultimately simple: Let's make this one short life we have really worth living. Let's put our petty problems at work into perspective and have the courage to solve them. Let's do it for the business, for the sake of those we care for, for the sake of our own mental and physical well-being and that of our colleagues. The stakes could not be higher.

# BIBLIOGRAPHY

Preface:

Sherwood, J.J. and Hoylman, F.M. (1977) *Utilizing Human Resources: Individual Approaches to Problem-solving and Decision-making.* Institute for research in the Behavioural, Economic and Management Sciences, paper no 621, Purdue University.

Chapter 1: The Inner Warrior

Seligman, M.E.P. (1974) Depression and learned helplessness. In R.J. Friedman and M.M. Katz (eds) *The Psychology of Depression: Contemporary Theory and Research.* Washington, DC: Winston-Wiley.

Chapter 2: The Gulliver Effect

Furnham, A. (2003) Article in *Sunday Times* (Sunday, September 7, 2003).
Hussey, D.E. (1998) *Managing Change.* London: Kogan Page.
Kotter, J.P., Schlesinger, A. and Sathe, V. (1986) *Organisational Readings in Organisational Design and Change.* Homewood, IL: Irwin.
Thomas, D.W. and Kilmann, R.H. (1974) *The Thomas–Kilmann Conflict Mode Instrument.* Palo Alto, CA: Consulting Psychologists Press.

Chapter 3: Developing Individuals: The Six Cs

Argyris, C. (1973) Some limits of rational man organizational theory, *Public Administration Review*, **33**(3): 253–67.
Belbin, R.M. (1993) *Team Roles at Work*, Butterworth Heinemann.
Hackman, J.R. and Lawler, E.E. (1971) Employee reactions to job characteristics, *Journal of Applied Psychology*, **55**(2): 259–86.
McClelland, D.C. and Burnham, D.H. (1995) Power is the great motivator, *Harvard Business Review*, **73**(1): 126–39 (first published in 1976).

Maier, N.R.F. (1970) *Problem Solving and Creativity in Individuals and Groups*. Belmont, CA: Brooks/Cole.

Rollinson, D. (2002) *Organizational Behaviour and Analysis: An Integrated Approach*, Pearson Education Limited.

## Chapter 4: Current Change Remedies

Beer, M. and Walton, A.L. (1987) 'Organization change and development', *Annual Review of Psychology*, **38**: 339–67.

Coch, L. and French, J.R.P. (1948) 'Overcoming resistance to change', *Human Relations*, **1**: 212–32.

Collins, D. (1998) *Organizational Change: Sociological Perspectives*. London: Routledge

Cunningham, I., Hyman, J. and Baldry, C. (1996) 'Empowerment: the power to do what?' *Industrial Relations Journal*, **27**(2):143–54.

Davenport, T. (1992) *Process Innovation: Re-engineering Work Through Information Technology*. Cambridge, MA: Harvard Business School Press.

Dawson, P. (1994) *Organizational Change: A Processual Approach*. London: Chapman.

Easton, G.S. (1993) 'The 1993 state of US Total Quality Management', *California Management Review*, Spring: 32–54.

French, W.L. and Bell, C.H. (1999) *Organization Development: Behavioural Science Interventions for Organizational Improvement*, 6th edn. Englewood Cliffs, NJ: Prentice Hall.

Golden, Jr W.P. (1972) 'On Becoming a Trainer' in W.G. Dyer, (ed.) *Modern Theory and Method in Group Training*. New York: Van Nostrand Reinhold.

Grey, C. and Mitev, M. (1995) Re-engineering organizations: a critical appraisal, *Personnel Review*, **24**(1): 6–18.

Hammer, M. and Champy, J. (1993) *Reengineering the Corporation: A Manifesto for Business Transformation*. New York: Brearley.

Holbech, L. (1994) *Career Development in Flatter Structures*. Horsham: Roffey Park Management Centre.

Luthans, F. (1993) 'Meeting the new paradigm changes through Total Quality Management', *Management Quarterly*, Spring: 2–13.

Macduffie, J.P. (1995) 'Human resource bundles and manufacturing performance: organizational logic and flexible production systems in the world auto industry', *Industrial and Labor Relations Review*, **48**(2): 107–28.

Rogers, E.M. (1993) *Communication of Innovations*, 3rd ed. New York: Free Press.

Stone, B. (1997) *Confronting Company Politics*. Basingstoke: Palgrave Macmillan.

Terpstra, D.E. (1981) 'Relationship between methodological rigour and reported outcomes in organizational development research', *Journal of Applied Psychology*, **66**(3): 541–3.

Woodman R.W. and Sherwood, J.J. (1980) 'The role of team development in organizational effectiveness: a critical review', *Psychological Bulletin*, **92**(2): 166–86.

## Chapter 5: On Becoming a Warrior

Beckhard, R. (1969) *Organisation Development: Its Nature, Origins and Prospects*. Reading, MA: Addison-Wesley.

Blake, R.R. and Mouton, S.R. (1983) *Consultation: A Handbook for Individual and Organisation Development*. Reading, MA: Addison-Wesley.

Cockman, P., Evans, B. and Reynolds, P. (1999) *Consulting for Real People*, 2nd edn. McGraw-Hill.

Swift, J. (2003) *Gulliver's Travels*, Penguin Classics (first published 1726).

## Chapter 6: Compassionate Leadership

Adair, J. (1986) *Effective Teambuilding*. Aldershot: Gower.

Barron, R.A. and Greenberg, J. (1990) *Behaviour in Organisations*. Needham Heights, MA: Allyn & Bacon.

Brightman, H. (2002) *GSU Master Teacher Program: On Learning Styles* www.gsu.edu/dschjb/wwwmbti.html.

Birkinshaw, J. and Crainer, S. (2002) *Leadership the Sven-Göran Eriksson Way*, Capstone.

Deloitte-Touche Human Capital Survey (January 2003) *Time To Deliver*, www.humanresourcesmagazine.com.

Goffee, R. and Jones, G., quoted in Birkinshaw, J. and Crainer, S. (2002) *Leadership the Sven-Göran Eriksson Way*, Capstone.

Goleman, D. (1995) *Emotional Intelligence: Why It Can Matter More Than IQ*. London: Bloomsbury.

Kiersey, D. and Bates, M. (1984) *Please Understand Me,* Prometheus Nemesis Book Company.

Kotter, J.P. (1988) *The Leadership Process*. New York: Free Press.

Leavitt, H.J. (1975) Beyond the Analytical Manager, *California Management Review*, **XVII**(4): 11–21.

McCourt, W. (1997) Discussion note: using metaphors to understand and to change organizations: a critique of Gareth Morgan's approach, *Organisation Studies,* **18**(3): 511–22.

McGregor, D. (1987) *The Human Side of Enterprise.* Harmondsworth: Penguin.

Margerison, C.J. and Lewis, R. (1981) 'Mapping managerial styles', *International Journal of Manpower*, Special Issue, **2**(1).

Mintzberg, H. (1976) Planning on the left side, managing on the right, *Harvard Business Review*, July–August, 49–58.

Morris, J., Potter. J. and Hooper, A. (1995) 'Effective Leaders at a Premium', *Professional Manager*, March, 26–8.

Myers, J.B. (1962) *The Myers-Briggs Type Indicator.* Princeton: Educational Testing Service.

OPP Ltd (2002) *Lessons in Leadership: A Research Report*, OPP Ltd.

Pearce, W. (1991) *Harvard Business Review,* quoted in *Leadership the Sven-Göran Eriksson Way*, Capstone (2002).

Rogers, C. (1961) *On Becoming a Person.* Boston, MA: Houghton Mifflin.

Rollinson, D. (2002) *Organizational Behaviour and Analysis: An Integrated Approach*, Pearson Education Limited.

## Chapter 7: Conflict

Thomas, D.W. and Kilmann, R.H. (1974) *The Thomas–Kilmann Conflict Mode Instrument.* Palo Alto, CA: Consulting Psychologists Press.

## Chapter 8: Concepts

Blake, R.R. and Mouton, S.R. (1983) *Consultation: A Handbook for Individual and Organisation Development.* Reading, MA: Addison-Wesley.

Kindred, M. (1987) *Once upon a group...* Published by Michael Kindred, ISBN 0-9512552-0-7.

## Chapter 12: Courage

Perls, F. (1971) *Gestalt Therapy Verbatim.* New York: Bantam Books.

Rabbi Susya, (1965) cited in Friedman, M. *Introduction to Martin Buber: Between Man and Man.* New York: Macmillan.

Yalom, I. (1980) *Existential Psychotherapy.* New York: Basic Books.

## Chapter 13: Embedding Courage Awareness

French, J.R.P. and Caplan, R.D. (1973) Organisational stress and individual strain. In A. J. Marrow (ed.) *The Failure of Success.* New York: AMACOM.

Lassey, W.R. and Sashkin, M. (eds) (1983) *Leadership and Social Change*, 3rd edn. San Diego, CA: University Associates (out of print).

Margolis, B.L., Kroes, W.H. and Quinn, R.P. (1974) Job Stress: an unlisted occupational health hazard, *Journal of Occupational Medicine,* **16**(4): 654–61.

# INDEX

Page numbers in **bold** type refer to figures; those in *italics* to tables

# Index

*Further information:*

If you would like to discuss the ideas in this book or to know more about Beverley Stone's work, please contact:

Email: Bev.Stone@virgin.net
Website: www.BevStone.com